MILITARY POWER

U.S. AIR FORCE SPECIAL OPS

FRED J. PUSHIES

ZENITH PRESS

To the Air Commandos
Past, Present, and Future

First published in 2007 by MBI Publishing Company LLC
and Zenith Press, an imprint of MBI Publishing Company,
Galtier Plaza, Suite 200, 380 Jackson Street, St. Paul, MN
55101 USA

The information in this book is true and complete to the best of
our knowledge. All recommendations are made without any
guarantee on the part of the author or Publisher, who also disclaim
any liability incurred in connection with the use of this data or
specific details.

This publication has been prepared solely by MBI Publishing
Company and is not approved or licensed by any other entity.
We recognize that some words, model names, and designations
mentioned herein are the property of the trademark holder. We
use them for identification purposes only. This is not an official
publication.

Zenith Press titles are also available at discounts in bulk quantity
for industrial or sales-promotional use. For details write to
Special Sales Manager at MBI Publishing Company, Galtier Plaza,
Suite 200, 380 Jackson Street, St. Paul, MN 55101 USA.

To find out more about our books, join us online at
www.zenithpress.com.

Library of Congress Cataloging-in-Publication Data
Pushies, Fred J., 1952-
   U.S. Air Force Special Ops / by Fred J. Pushies. — [Rev. ed.].
      p. cm.
   Includes index.
   ISBN-13: 978-0-7603-2947-4 (softbound)
   ISBN-10: 0-7603-2947-8 (softbound)
   1. United States. Air Force Special Operations Command—
History. 2. Special forces (Military science)—United States—
History. 3. United States. Air Force—Commando troops. I. Title.
II. Title: USAF Special Ops. III. Title: U.S. Air Force Special
Operations.
   UG633.P87 2007
   358.4—dc22   2006038828

On the front cover: The MH-53J Pave Low is a modified version
of the HH-53 Super Jolly Green Giant helicopter used extensively
during the Vietnam War for special operations and rescue of
combat personnel. During past space programs, the HH-53
was on duty at the launch site as the primary astronaut recovery
vehicle. Under the Air Force's Pave Low IIIE program, nine
MH-53H's and thirty two HH-53s were modified for night and
adverse weather operations and designated MH-53J's. Their
modifications included forward-looking infrared, GPS, Doppler
navigation systems, a terrain-following and terrain-avoidance radar,
an on-board computer, and integrated avionics to enable precise
navigation to and from target areas. *U.S. Air Force*

On the frontispiece: AFSOC logo. *U.S. Air Force*

On the title page: At a classified airfield in Afghanistan, Humvee
vehicle is loaded onto a MC-130P Combat Shadow.
This scene would be repeated over and over as AFSOC aircrews
inserted U.S. Special Operations forces through their area of
operations as they hunted down Taliban and al-Qaeda fighters.
Capable of landing in the dark, most likely the landing zone
would already be marked out by a waiting special tactics team.
U.S. Air Force

On the back cover: U.S. Air Force combat controllers gear-up for
a night-fire exercise at a forward-deployed location supporting
Operation Enduring Freedom. Combat controllers conduct and
support special operations missions under clandestine, covert, or
low-visibility conditions. *U.S. Air Force*

About the Author
Fred J. Pushies has spent the last sixteen years in the company of
each of the units assigned to United States Special Operations
Command (SOCOM). He has skimmed across the waves with
the SEALs in an eighty-two foot long Mark V Special Operations
craft, flown at treetop level with the 160th Special Operations
Aviation Regiment, and crunched through the brush with Force
Recon Marines. His integrity and insight are evident in his
previous works, *Special Ops: America's Elite Forces in 21st Century
Combat, U.S. Air Force Special Ops, U.S. Army Special Forces, Marine
Force Recon,* and *Weapons of the U.S. Navy SEALs.*

Editor: Steve Gansen
Designer: LeAnn Kuhlmann

Printed in China

Contents

Acknowledgments

First, I want to thank God that we live in a country where freedom and liberty are more than concepts: they are our way of life. A special thanks to the men and women of AFSOC who put it on the line daily to keep it that way. I thank the following individuals for their assistance in making this book possible: Steve Gansen, editor, MBI Publishing; Matt Durham (LTC-ret); Lt. Col. Stephanie Holcombe; Sandy Henry; Capt. Darren Berry, Capt. Elizabeth Paul, Major Erin Dick, Capt. Tom Montgomery, Air Force Special Operations Command (AFSOC), Public Affairs Office; Capt. Charles Stoner and AC-130U crew, Capt. Kevin Huber, Capt. Cheree Kochen, Capt. Derrek Price, 4th Special Operations Squadron (SOS); Lt. Col. Tim Shaffer, 4th SOS; the Pave Low crews of the 20th SOS, the Green Hornets; Capt. Tom Dermody, Capt. Chris Lambert, Staff Sgt. Donny Wright, Technical Sgt. Eddie Linnbaum, Technical Sgt. Robert Smith, Senior Airman Brian McDaniel; Col. Ken Rodriguez; Major Michael Sneeder; Capt. Frankie Rodriguez, Staff Sgt. Bob Benton and team, the 23rd Special Tactics Squadron (STS); Staff Sgt. Terry Saltzman, Senior Airman John Chilcoat, Master Sgt. "Andy," Technical Sgt. "Brad," Technical Sgt. "Mike," Wayne Norad (CSM-ret.); Mr. Herb Mason; Charlie Jones, Chief Warrant Officer (ret.), Air Commando Association; Capt. Kris Koller, 193rd SOS; Capt. Gideon McClure, AETC/PAN; Oscar Balladares, Lackland AFB; Mr. Ron Childress, Master Sgt. (ret.); Technical Sgt. Bart Decker, Technical Sgt. Dirk Wenrich, and Staff Sgt. Rick Driggers; Crew of "Niner-One-Niner," MC-130 Papa Duke Air Force Base; Robert Genat; Lt. M. Chavis, 324 TRS; Monica Manganero, Fort Benning PAO; Carol Darby, USASOC PAO, Fort Bragg; John Satterfield, Doug Kinneard, Boeing; Mr. Ola Bericksing, Borfors, Sweden; Chief Master Sgt. Paul Venturella, Combat Control School, Pope Air Force Base; Irene Witt, 37th Training Wing PAO; Master Sgt. Douglas Issacks, 342 TRS/CFT; Garry Lewry, PJ/CRO Training Manager, Command Sgt. Evans Everett, Commandant, PJ/CRO School 342 TRS, Major Anthony Capobianco, 342 TRS/CC; 1st Lt. Kevin Kirby, TRS/ADO; Robert McLucas, Squadron Leader, RAF 342 TRS/DO, Staff Sgt. Anna Castillo 37 TRG/CCEA; Capt. Barb Carson, Kirtland Air Force Base PAO; Master Sgt. David Lee and Master Sgt. Rick Weaver, Pararescue School, Kirtland Air Force Base; Sue Webster, Jamie Wagler, Naval Surface Warfare Center—Crane; Ensign Joe Vermetleo, CENTCOM Public Affairs Office; David Lutz, Vice President Military Operations, Knight's Armament Company; Angela Harrell, Phil DeGaris, Heckler & Koch Defense division; David Hale, Insight Technology, Inc.; Timothy M. Jensen, Rockwell; Gene Adcock, Night Vision Equipment Company; Barbara Sadowy, FHN USA and Kimberly Kasitz, General Atomics Aeronautical Systems, Inc.; Van Donohue, Vice President Sales and Marketing, Michael Curlett, Director of European Sales, and John Bailey, EOTech; and Timothy Ford, President, Adventure Lights.

I also say thanks to my daughters, Jennifer and Julie, for their support of this project and especially to my wife, Tammy, for holding down the fort while I was out skimming the tree-tops in Pave Lows and crunching through the brush with the special tactics teams.

Chapter 1

THE QUIET PROFESSIONALS

A clandestine MC-130H Combat Talon II glides through the slipstream at twenty-five thousand feet above enemy territory, its forward-looking infrared and array of electronic equipment constantly on the lookout for hostiles. Time hack, 0215; the pilot brings the aircraft to twelve thousand feet. An arm shoots up into the air and the nomex-gloved hand spreads out, signaling to the team they are five minutes from the insertion point.

Moments later the rear cargo ramp is lowered and three heavily laden figures in battle dress uniform (BDU) and parachutes approach the opening. They huddle together like an NFL team before the final play of the game. Last-minute checks are made, and equipment is tugged one more time. One member reaches down and gives a reassuring pat to the M4A1 carbine with suppressor attached to his harness; another glances one last time at his altimeter.

GREEN … GREEN … GREEN, the jump light flashes and in a heartbeat all three men, as one, hurl themselves into the dark abyss that waits for them. Assuming a stable free-fall position, they are plummeting to the earth's surface, now eleven thousand feet below, at approximately two hundred feet per second. The only sound heard is their breathing through the oxygen masks and the wind as it tears at their bodies and equipment. Moments turn into an eternity; then it is time. The altimeter now dictates that they transcend from their lofty flight and prepare to engage their RAPS, or ram-air parachute system. One final check of the altimeter and compass. As they reach the thirty-five hundred–foot point, one after the other pulls on the rip cord. Only the sounds of the canopy foils being deployed are heard by the team. In little more than two minutes after leaving the aircraft, they are ready to steer toward their landing zone.

The landing zone (LZ) is about the size of a basketball court, and each of the men perform stand-up landings as they hit the target. They quickly remove their chutes and bring their weapons up to the ready positions. Silently the point man moves up onto a rocky crag. Stops. Listens. Surveys the area. Listens again. After he is satisfied that they have arrived undetected, he directs his attention back to the rest of the team and with a deliberate, silent hand motion signals to them to converge on the point man's position.

The team leader pulls out a global positioning system (GPS) and verifies the location and direction to the target. The information is passed on to the point man who sets a compass heading and heads out. The team moves through the mountainous terrain and scraggly trees like an invisible zephyr.

After traveling more than an hour, the team assumes a potion atop a ridgeline, where they begin to break out their equipment. An AN/PRC-117F radio is pulled from one rucksack, from another a SATCOM antennae. A few feet away a Special Operations forces laser aiming module is set up. While this high-tech gear is being set up, the other team member provides security with his MK46 machinegun. With two hundred rounds of linked 7.62mm ammunition, he is ready to defend the team's position.

The team settles in, but their wait is not long. The intelligence from the local contact is right on, and soon winding down the mountain pass below them is a convoy of Toyota pickup trucks. Using night-vision equipment, the team leader verifies the al-Qaeda target and gives a nod to "paint" the lead vehicle. The SOFLAM begins to emit a chirping as the operator holds the cross hairs on the four-wheel-drive pickup. The seconds tick by, then out of an ebony sky a five hundred–pound MK-82 bomb homes in on the lead vehicle, turning the night into day, as flames streak skyward. Before the trail vehicle can turn around, another MK-82 converts it into scrap metal. With the three middle trucks now trapped in between, the occupants leap from the vehicles, but there is nowhere to hide, as overhead an AC-130U "Spooky" gunship metes out death from its 40mm Bofors and 25mm Gatling gun.

Left: One of the Pave Low's gunners readies the M2 .50-caliber machine gun. With a shell more than five inches in length, it is a formidable weapon against troops, bunkers, and soft-skinned vehicles, such as APCs.

Before the echo fades from the night, the team has already packed up and radioed for extraction. Just as the last man shoulders his rucksack, there is a familiar sound of rotor blades beating against the night air, as an MH-53 Pave Low looms out of the darkness. Their mission complete, the team loads onto the huge helicopter and heads back to the forward operation base (FOB).

Who are these men?

They are not U.S. Navy SEALs, but they may have marked the area with infra-beacons before the frogmen fast-roped in. They are not U.S. Army Rangers, but before the Rangers ever executed an air drop on a drop zone this team might have been there for days.

You will not see them depicted in movies with guns blazing or as the main characters in the latest Clancy novel. They prefer their anonymity and are often the unsung heroes of many covert operations. They are the men of the U.S. Air Force Special Operations Command, the Air Commandos, the Quiet Professionals. Their motto: ANYTIME, ANYWHERE.

The origins of these Quiet Professionals can be traced back to the beginning of World War II. Aircrews and aircraft were used in the clandestine, unconventional, and psychological warfare roles in both the European and Pacific theaters of operation.

The Combat Talon of today would find its forerunner in the highly modified, paint-blackened B-24 "Liberator" bombers. These specialized B-24s were flown by members of the 801st Bombardment Group, Army Air Corps who were known as the Carpetbaggers. The crews of this unit, much like their current descendants, became proficient in flying low-level, long-range missions in terrain that was mostly

The bomber was operated by the 801st Bombardment Group, nicknamed the "Carpetbaggers." This group specialized in covert air operations. An ancestor of today's Combat Talons, operating mostly at night, these highly modified, black-painted aircraft were utilized in the delivery of supplies, OSS agents, and leaflets behind enemy lines in Europe. *AFSOC*

mountains in poor weather and, of course, at night. These planes were instrumental in the delivery of covert agents, supplies, and psychological leaflets behind the enemy's lines.

The agents who would be parachuted into enemy-held territory were members of the Office of Strategic Services (OSS). Known as Jedburgh teams, these teams generally consisted of three men and would link up with the partisan resistance fighters and organize and conduct guerrilla operations against the Germans in preparation of Operation Overlord.

In the early part of June 1944, six Jedburgh teams were parachuted into strategic locations in Brittany and France. There, units were successful in relaying critically needed intelligence in preparation for the Allied invasion of Normandy, on 6 June 1944—D-day.

On another occasion, Air Corps special operations aircrews were tasked with the insertion of OSS agents into Yugoslavia, codename Halyard Mission. These agents, in connection with the partisans, arranged for the return of downed aircrews. Between June and August 1944 these OSS teams, along with help from the partisans, recovered more than four hundred Americans and eighty Allied personnel. They were transported out on Air Corps C-47 transports from covert airfields.

World War II in the Pacific

While the OSS Jedburgh Teams were successfully conducting guerrilla operations in Europe, other aircrews were earning their namesake in the Pacific.

On 26 August 1943, Gen. Henry H. "Hap" Arnold held a meeting with British Admiral Lord Louis Mountbatten to review plans for American air assistance of British commando operations in the China-Burma-India theater of operations. It was during this time that General Arnold brought into being the concept of a new force, a highly mobile fighting unit, complete with its own transportation and logistics. This unit, which would exhibit the "can-do" spirit, would evolve into the No. 1 Air Commando Group. General Arnold used the term "air commando" to honor Lord Mountbatten, who had previously commanded British commandos.

During its formation, this unit was initially designated Project 9, then Project CA 281. Later the name was changed

to the 5318th Provisional Unit (Air), then once again to No. 1 Air Commando Force, and finally, the 1st Air Commando Group (1 ACG) in March 1944.

The task of forming this unit fell upon two veteran fighter pilots, Lieutenant Colonels Philip G. Cochran and John R. Alison. They were to build a self-sufficient, highly motivated combat unit to support British Brig. Gen. Orde C. Wingate and his "Chindits" on long-range infiltrations into Burma, opposing the Japanese.

Cochran and Alison were designated co-commanders and given carte blanche by General Arnold. Their orders were simple: ". . . I want the USAAF to spearhead General Wingate's operation." Then the general gave them a further admonition: "To hell with the paperwork, go out and fight."

For such an organization, there was no table of organization and equipment (TO&E). Under the highest priority given to them by General Arnold, they were able to obtain the needed men and supplies to create the unit.

The task of manning the unit fell to Capt. Robert E. Moist. Due to the covert nature of their mission, prospective candidates were given a minimal amount of information. No information regarding destination, but they were assured that missions would include combat. The attraction of combat and secrecy of the missions was enough to fill the ranks and made recruiting easy. In keeping with the nature of secrecy, the unit adopted the unofficial patch of a black question mark on a white circle.

With the manpower problem solved, Cochran and Alison now directed their attention to the aircraft needed to accomplish their mission. The inventory of aircraft grew, and soon they had at their disposal C-47 Dakota Transports, CG-4A Waco gliders, P-51 Mustangs and P-47 Thunderbolt fighters, B-25 Mitchell bombers, UC-64 Norseman utility aircraft, L-1 Vigilant and L-5 Sentinel liaison planes, and for the first time in a combat environment, the YR-4 helicopter.

The air commandos flew over hazardous mountains and jungles to find and resupply the highly mobile British ground forces in hostile territory. Their success eventually led to the creation of two other such groups, the 2nd and 3rd ACGs.

The mission of the 1st Air Commando Group as defined by General Arnold was to facilitate the forward movement of

11

Wingate's troops, to supply and evacuate Wingate's force, to provide limited air covering and striking force, and to acquire air experience under the conditions expected to be encountered.

Arnold's air commandos performed a variety of conventional and unconventional combat as well as support missions deep behind enemy lines. The air commandos are credited with the first combat aircrew rescue by helicopter, multiple ground targets destroyed, and a number of enemy aircraft shot down.

On 15 February 1944, during a night training mission, an accident involving a C-47 Dakota and two Waco gliders took the lives of four of Wingate's men as well as three Americans.

Such an incident could have easily shaken the men of the British force. On the following day, however, Wingate's commander sent a note to the air commandos reassuring their faith and trust in the unit's capability. The note read, "Please be assured that we will go with your boys Any Place, Any Time, Any Where." This phrase became the motto of the 1st Air Commando Group and has been used in one variation or another in subsequent Air Commando units as well as by today's Air Force Special Operations Command.

Post–World War II and Korea

With the end of World War II the U.S. military underwent many changes. The OSS evolved into the Central Intelligence Agency (CIA). The Army Air Corps became the U.S. Air Force, and the Air Commando Group was officially deactivated.

Officially, the U.S. Air Force no longer had an unconventional warfare capability. Unofficially, however, with the entrance of the United States into the Korean War, the USAF found itself again running clandestine operations, this time for the newly formed CIA. Under direction of the Military Air Transport Service (MATS), the Air Resupply and Communications Service (ARCS) was created on 28 February 1951. ARCS would be responsible for many of the covert operations of the war.

As their predecessors before them in World War II, those who flew and fought in Korea would pass along the heritage as they passed along their addition to the Air Commando legacy.

Cold War Era

With the end of the Korean War, the primary mission of the U.S. Air Force would be that of land-based bombers and intercontinental ballistic missiles of the Strategic Air Command. Once again, the U.S. Air Force's special operation would silently slip away into the shadows, until needed. Throughout the 1950s the U.S. Air Force was tasked with supporting anti-Communist rebellions.

Vietnam

Early on in the sixties, the Cold War began to heat up, primarily in Third World countries where Communist-led insurgents introduced a violent movement to those areas. Known as "Wars of Liberation," they sprung up all around the globe. Obviously, this caused great concern in the United States and other Western nations.

President John F. Kennedy had developed an interest in counterinsurgency, the method of defeating guerrilla movements. He would go on to say, "There is another type of war, new in its intensity, ancient in its origins—war by guerrillas, subversives, insurgents, assassins, war by ambush instead of combat. . . ." President Kennedy recognized a need for a force, a "special" force to counter this threat.

The U.S. Air Force response came in the spring of 1961, when Gen. Curtis E. LeMay, Air Force Chief of Staff, directed the creation of the 4400th Combat Crew Training Squadron (CCTS), codename "Jungle Jim." Located at Eglin Air Force Base, Auxiliary Field No. 9 (Hurlburt Field), the 4400th CCTS started its journey into the annals of Special Warfare history with 352 officers and men and a total inventory of thirty-two aircraft (sixteen C-47 transports, eight B-26 bombers, and eight T-28 trainers).

The mission of the 4400th CCTS was to provide close air support for Special Forces behind enemy lines and counterinsurgency training. The CCTS developed foreign internal defense (FID) tactics and techniques for building a counterinsurgency capability in numerous Third World countries.

Later that year, in November 1961, Detachment 2 of the 4400th CCTS, codename "Farm Gate," deployed to the Republic of South Vietnam. They were to become the first U.S. Air Force unit to conduct actual combat operations in

A Fulton recovery balloon breaks away from an MC-130E Combat Talon aircraft during an interception. This device, known as a "Skyhook," allowed the extraction of Special Operations forces teams. Up to five hundred pounds of personnel and equipment could be attached to a balloon via a nylon line. As the Combat Talon approached, the yoke arms or "whiskers" were extended to snag the line. The balloon would then break away and the line would feed into an attached power winch in the rear of the aircraft. The individuals or cargo would then be reeled into the aircraft via the ramp door. *U.S. Air Force*

Vietnam. As the war in Vietnam expanded, so did the role of the U.S. Air Force's Special Operations forces. General LeMay responded to this in the expansion of the 4400th CCTS to the Special Air Warfare Center (SAWC) at Eglin in April 1962. SAWC consisted of the 1st Air Commando Group, 1st Air Combat Applications Group, and a combat support group. To assist the new organization, the air force created a new "counterinsurgency" office specialty code.

In May 1963, the 1st Air Commando Group was redesignated the 1st Air Commando Wing. Operational strength rose from 2,665 to 3,000 and the squadrons increased to six. In the tradition of their predecessors, the Vietnam-era Air Commandos developed tactics and techniques that earned their exploits an honored place in Air Force Special Operations heritage. Their dedication and courage was recognized in the fact that out of the twelve U.S. Air Force Medals of Honor, five would be awarded to members of the Air Force Special Operations.

As the Vietnam War began winding down, SOF capability progressively declined as well. In June 1974, USAFSOF was redesignated the 834th Tactical Composite Wing (TCW), effectively bringing to a close the most aggressive, far-reaching effort by the USAF to support unconventional warfare. In July 1975, the 834th TCW was renamed the 1st Special Operations Wing (1 SOW), and by 1979 it was the only SOF wing.

Chapter 2

THE ORIGIN OF AIR FORCE SPECIAL OPS

What began as a noble attempt by the U.S. Special Operations forces ended in tragedy in the darkness of an Iranian desert. It was April 1980 when Special Forces Operation Detachment Delta, better known as "Delta Force," along with its U.S. Air Force and marine aircrews, met with disaster. What Colonel "Charging" Charlie Beckwith did not know at the time was that the operation was headed toward disaster from the onset. Over the years there have been investigations, hearings, and countless articles written on why the mission ended in a debacle, so we will not belabor the issue here. All the Monday-morning quarterbacks had one conclusion in common, however, Operation Eagle Claw failed. This cost the lives of eight gallant troops, it cost the honor of the United States of America, and it hurt the credibility of U.S. special operations.

The U.S. Navy helicopters with marine pilots proved to be the Achilles' heel of Operation Eagle Claw. One can only speculate on the compilations of mishaps that besieged the Sea Stallion helicopters. Some got lost in the desert and others malfunctioned, leaving the anxious force without the adequate airlift capability necessary to accomplish the rescue attempt. From the inception of the plan they were "the" weak link. Were the pilots up to the task?

The marine pilots, if we look at today's standards, had big boots to fill. They were being asked to fly at night. This alone was unusual practice for the "flying leathernecks." These pilots were now being asked to perform the extraordinary: launch off the deck of a carrier, at night, fly NOE (nape of the earth) where radar could not detect them, and use no running lights. The pilots were issued PVS5 night-vision goggles; however, they could be worn only at thirty-minute intervals. This meant the pilot and co-pilot had to alternate flying the huge helicopter every thirty minutes. The marines had no pilots that had been trained in this type of flying. In fact, none of the service branches were prepared for such a contingency.

Following the disaster at Desert One, a review committee known as the Holloway Commission convened to look into problems within U.S. special operations. The outcome of this commission resulted in two major recommendations. First, that the Department of Defense should establish a counterterrorism task force (CTJTF) as a field organization of the Joint Chiefs of Staff (JCS) with a permanently assigned staff and forces. The JCS would plan, train for, and conduct operations to counter terrorist activities against the United States. The CTJTF would use military forces in the counterterrorism (CT) role. These forces could range in size from small units of highly specialized personnel to larger integrated forces. Second, the JCS should consider the formation of a Special Operations Advisory Panel (SOAP). This panel would consist of high-ranking officers to be drawn from both active service and retired personnel. The prerequisite for selection was a background in special operations or having served as a commander in chief (CINC) or JCS level and having maintained a proficient level of interest in special operations or defense policy.

The mission of the SOAP would be to review and evaluate highly classified special operations planning to provide an independent assessment. Consequently, the progressive reorganization and resurgence of U.S. Special Operations forces began.

While this was occurring, the U.S. Air Force transferred responsibility for Air Force Special Operations from Tactical Air Command (TAC) to Military Airlift Command (MAC) in December 1982. The commander of the 23rd Air Force at Scott Air Force Base, Illinois, would assume all control of the Air Force Special Operations units. This new numbered U.S. Air Force was tasked with the worldwide missions of special

Left: In addition to providing air support for U.S. Special Operations forces, AFSOC would provide ATC and pararescue capabilities for USSOCOM. Here, Staff Sgt. Bob Benton of the 23rd Special Tactics Squadron, pauses and watches over his team as they take a break from patrolling through the dense jungle. He is armed with a GUU-5/P assault rifle with M203 40mm grenade launcher in hand, ready for instant use, should the need arise.

An HC-130 Hercules refuels two of the 20th Special Operations Squadron's HH-53 helicopters. These forerunners of today's MH-53 Pave Low helicopters are officially known as Sea Stallions but were nicknamed "Super Jolly Green Giants" or "Super Jollies" for their large green airframes. Marine-flown variants comprised the rotary wing element of Operation Eagle Claw. While there were numerous factors leading to the devastating failure of the operation, one of the most significant was the range of the helicopters. It was clear that U.S. Special Operations forces needed longer range heliborne capability for the insertion and extraction of its operators. *U.S. Air Force*

operations, combat rescue, pararescue training, medical evacuation, and training of HC-130 and helicopter crewmen.

Subsequently, on 1 March 1983, in response to the Holloway Commission Report, all U.S. Air Force Special Operations forces were consolidated into the 1st Special Operations Wing (SOW) at Hurlburt Field, Florida. The 1st SOW would direct and coordinate active and reserve components of the Special Operation Squadrons (SOS). Active components consisted of the 8th SOS operating MC-130 Combat Talons and HC-130 Hercules tankers, the 16th SOS operating AC-130 Spectre gunships, and the 20th SOS operating the MH-53 Pave Low and HH-53 Jolly Green Giant helicopters. The 1720th Special Tactics Group provided the combat control teams.

Reserve components of U.S. Air Force Special Operations forces included the 919th Special Operations Group (SOG) operating AC-130A gunships, the 302nd SOG operating the EC-130E command and control aircraft, and the Pennsylvania Air National Guard flying the Volant Solo EC-130E psychological operations (PSYOP) aircraft.

In addition to traditional special operations skills, the 23rd conducted weather reconnaissance, security support for intercontinental ballistic missile sites, and training of USAF helicopter and HC-130 crewmen.

Operation Urgent Fury

In October 1983, 23rd AF participated with other Caribbean forces in the successful rescue of Americans from the island nation of Grenada. During the seven-day operation, centered at Point Salines Airport, 23rd AF furnished MC-130s, AC-130s, and EC-130 aircraft, aircrews, maintenance, and support people.

During the Grenada operation the 1st Special Operations Wing had two missions. MC-130 Combat Talons were tasked with delivering U.S. Army Rangers to Point Salines, while Spectre gunships provided the air-to-ground support fire. Combat controllers were air-dropped in with the U.S. Army Rangers at Port Salinas airport, making an unprecedented combat jump from only five hundred feet. Each controller was laden with parachute gear and more than ninety pounds of mission-critical equipment. Upon landing they quickly established a command and control radio net. They carried out air traffic operations for follow-on forces both at the airport and other in-country missions. In addition to this, the combat control teams (CCT) performed as forward air control (FAC) for U.S. Air Force Spectre gunships, Navy fighters, and Army helicopter gunships.

Throughout the operation the crews of the 1st SOW continued in the tradition of the Air Commandos who preceded them. Flying in numerous sorties and fire missions they performed mission after mission. During the entire operations, they sustained no casualties.

The Grenada operation was not without its cost to the special operations community. Four U.S. Navy SEALs were lost at sea during a Rubber Duck insertion. This tragedy hit the SOF community hard. Operation Urgent Fury was also fraught with planning problems from the get-go. A lack of standardization for the special operation assets contributed to this plan gone awry.

Special Operations forces in Grenada did have a few rough edges; however, most of these planning problems were overcome as the special operations personnel from all three service branches excelled at what they do best: improvise, adapt, and overcome to achieve their missions' goals.

The Grenada mission was the springboard for the further consolidation of U.S. Special Operations forces. The U.S. Air Force particularly took a proactive stance to rebuild a powerful special operations force. In May 1986, Congressman William Cohen, Senator Sam Nunn, and Congressman Dan Daniel introduced legislation that formed the basis to amend the 1986 Defense Authorizations Bill. This bill, signed into law in October 1986, in part directed the formation of a unified command responsible for special operations. In April 1987, the United States Special Operations Command (USSOCOM) was established at

Hurlburt Field, located west of Eglin AFB, is the home of the U.S. Air Force Special Operations Command.

MacDill Air Force Base, Florida, and U.S. Army Gen. James J. Lindsay assumed command. Four months later, 23rd Air Force moved to Hurlburt Field.

In August 1989, Gen. Duane H. Cassidy, MAC commander in chief, divested all nonspecial operations units from the 23rd Air Force. Consequently, the 23rd Air Force served in a dual role—reporting to MAC, but also functioning as the air component to USSOCOM.

Operation Just Cause

On 20 December 1989, at 0100 local, the United States launched an attack on Panama. The objectives of the attack were to protect U.S. personnel and installations, neutralize the Panamanian Defense Force, and capture Manuel Noriega. During this operation the Air Force Special Operations units saw extensive use. Due to the surgical firing capability, the AC-130 gunships were the ideal solution for the close-in urban combat environment with limited collateral damage. The gunships were launched from the 16th Special Operations Squadron ("Ghostriders") at Hurlburt Field, Florida.

Other Air Force Special Operations assets included an EC-130 from the 193rd ANG stationed at the Harrisburg Airport, Pennsylvania, to perform psychological warfare operations during the invasion. Pararescuemen and CCTs participated in operations with the U.S. Army's 75th Rangers at

Torrijos Airfield and Rio Hato Air Base. Combat controllers would also be attached to U.S. Navy SEAL Team 4 in support of the frogmen as they assaulted Paitilla Airport and disabled Noriega's personal jet.

In retrospect, Operation Just Cause served as a proving ground for the 1991 war in the Middle East. Night tactics and stealth weapons were battle tested in Panama and later accounted for many of the successes in Desert Storm. While not quite the fiasco of the Grenadian assault in 1983, Operation Just Cause did have some serious problems. Talk to the SEALs who survived the raid at Paitilla Airport. The invasion of Panama also established a strategy in the way U.S. Special Operations forces were deployed and used in the future.

The Birth of Air Force Special Operations Command (AFSOC)

On 22 May 1990, Gen. Larry D. Welch, U.S. Air Force Chief of Staff, redesignated 23rd Air Force as Air Force Special Operations Command (AFSOC). AFSOC became responsible for the combat readiness of Air Force Special Operations forces. Headquartered at Hurlburt Field, Florida, the group reports directly to the U.S. Air Force Chief of Staff

Subdued patch of the Air Force Special Operations Command.

and is the air force's component of the U.S. Special Operations Command.

The new major command consisted of three wings, the 1st, 39th, and 353rd Special Operations Wings, as well as the 1720th Special Tactics Group, the U.S. Air Force Special Operations School, and the Special Missions Operational Test and Evaluation Center. The Air Reserve components included the 919th Special Operations Group (U.S. Air Force Reserve) at Duke Field, Florida, and the 193rd SOG (Air National Guard) at Harrisburg Airport, Pennsylvania.

Today, having undergone further evolutions, AFSOC has approximately twenty thousand active, reserve, National Guard, and civilian personnel. The command owns more than 160 fixed- and rotary-wing aircraft, divided among one wing, the 16th SOW, and two groups, the 352nd and 353rd SOG. This configuration epitomizes the consolidated wing/group concept.

AFSOC is the U.S. Air Force element of the United States Special Operation Command (USSOCOM). Its mission is to provide mobility, surgical firepower, covert tanker support, and special tactics teams. These units will normally operate in concert with U.S. Army and U.S. Navy Special Operations forces, including Special Forces, Rangers, Special Operations Aviation Regiment, SEAL teams, PYSOP forces, and civil affairs units. AFSOC supports a wide range of activities from combat operations of a limited duration to longer-term conflicts. They also provide support to foreign governments and their military. Dependent on shifting priorities, AFSOC maintains a flexible profile allowing it to respond to numerous missions.

AFSOC is committed to continual improvement to provide Air Force Special Operations forces for worldwide deployment and assignment to regional linked commands to conduct unconventional warfare, direct action, special reconnaissance, personnel recovery, counterterrorism, foreign internal defense, psychological operations, and collateral special operations activities.

16th Special Operations Wing

Located at Hurlburt Field, the 16th Special Operations Wing is the oldest and most experienced unit in AFSOC. It includes: the 3rd SOS (Dragons), which flies the Predator unmanned aerial vehicle; the 4th SOS (Ghostriders), which operates the AC-130U Spooky gunships; the 6th Special Operations Squadron, which is responsible for the SOW's aviation foreign internal defense unit; the 8th SOS (Blackbirds), which flies the MC-130E Combat Talon; the 9th SOS (Night Wings) flying the MC-130E Combat Talon I; the 15th SOS, with the MC-130H Combat Talon II; the 16th SOS, equipped with the AC-130H Spectre gunship; the 319th SOS operating the U-28A aircraft, and the 20th SOS (Green Hornets), which flies the MH-53J Pave Low III helicopter.

In addition to Hurlburt Field, in June 2006 AFSOC began evaluation of Cannon Air Force Base, New Mexico, as the new home for an Air Force Special Operations wing, scheduled for October 2007. Due to the historical lineage, the 16th Special Operations Wing flag will transition to Cannon, and Hurlburt Field will regain its designation as the 1st Special Operations Wing. And will continue as the headquarters of Air Force Special Operations Command.

According to Lt. Gen. Michael W. Wooley, AFSOC commander, "The AFSOC expansion to Cannon offers special operators a western U.S. base to enhance support for its operations in the Pacific theater and to meet the objectives of our global defense posture. Additionally, the Melrose Range and the surrounding region open up new and unrestricted training opportunities AFSOC does not currently experience, to include joint and composite training with other services and nations, as well as mission training opportunities. Cannon basing of AFSOC assets enables the special operations community easy access to a high desert training environment much like that encountered in contingency operations."

The growth in AFSOC weapons systems and personnel will be divided between Hurlburt Field and Cannon AFB. New aircraft, including the CV-22 Osprey, will be assigned to

Members of the 6th SOS specialize in foreign internal defense to train, advise, and assist the air forces of foreign countries. While the majority of SOF pilots have transitioned to the "glass cockpit," the pilots assigned to the 6th remain proficient in the use of the old "steam gauges" of older aircraft; several imprinted in Russian or other languages. Their inventory includes vintage aircraft that they may encounter in a Third World country (e.g., old C-47 transports, Hueys, and an assortment of Soviet aircraft). *U.S. Air Force*

Hurlburt/Eglin as well as to the new wing at Cannon. Other potential aircraft for Cannon are AC-130U Gunships and the MC-130H Combat Talon II. As of this writing the final aircraft mix between Cannon and Hurlburt Field has not been finalized.

352nd Special Operations Group

Stationed overseas at RAF Mildenhall, United Kingdom is the designated U.S. Air Force component for Special Operations Command Europe. Its squadrons are the 7th SOS, which flies the MC-130H Combat Talon II; the 21st SOS, equipped with the MH-53J Pave Low; and the 67th SOS, with the HC-130N/P Combat Shadow and the 321st Special Tactics Squadron.

353rd Special Operations Group

Residing at Kadena Air Base, Japan, is the U.S. Air Force component for Special Operations Command Pacific. The squadrons are the 1st SOS, which flies the MC-130E Combat Talon I; the 17th SOS, with the MC-130N/P Combat Shadow; and the 31st SOS at Osan Air Base, Korea, which flies the MH-53J Pave Low III helicopter.

720th Special Tactics Group

Headquartered at Hurlburt Field, the 720th Special Tactics Group has units in the United States, Europe, and the Pacific. The group has special operations combat control teams and pararescue forces. Their missions include air traffic control for establishing air assault landing zones, close air support for strike aircraft and Spectre gunship missions, establishing casualty collection stations, and providing trauma care for injured personnel.

Its squadrons include the 21st STS at Pope Air Force Base, North Carolina; 22nd STS at McChord Air Force Base, Washington; 23rd STS at Hurlburt Field; the 24th STS located at Fort Bragg, North Carolina; and the 10th Combat Weather Squadron at Hurlburt Field.

Air Force Special Operations School

Reporting directly to AFSOC and at Hurlburt Field, the school provides special operations–related education to Department of Defense personnel, government agencies, and allied nations. More than seven thousand students attend the school each year.

Activated in April 1967, the USAF Special Air Warfare School was located at Eglin Air Force Base. In 1968 it was redesignated the USAF Special Operations School. It was in 1987 when the school, then under the command of the 23rd Air Force, was assigned to the U.S. Special Operations Command (USSOCOM) at MacDill Air Force Base, Tampa, Florida. On 22 May 1990 the school became a direct report of the newly established Air Force Special Operations Command (AFSOC) at Hurlburt Field.

Curriculum enhances the mission readiness and force survivability. Subjects covered in its eighteen courses include introduction to special operations, regional affairs, cross-cultural communications, antiterrorism awareness, revolutionary warfare, joint psychological operations, joint special operations planning, joint aviation's foreign internal defense, and other classified areas.

18th Flight Test Squadron

With headquarters at Hurlburt Field, the 18th Flight Test Squadron conducts operational and maintenance suitability tests and evaluations for equipment, concepts, tactics, and procedures for employment of Special Operations forces. Many of these tests are joint command and joint service projects.

919th Special Operations Wing
(U.S. Air Force Reserve)

The 919th Special Operations Wing is located at Duke Field, Florida, whose 711th SOS—which once flew the AC-130A gunships—have been transitioned over to the MC-130E Combat Talon I. The squadron trains in the deployment of Special Operations forces or mission-critical equipment, day or night, at low levels into denied or hostile areas of operations. The 5th SOS flies the HC-130N/P Combat Shadow tanker. This unit flies clandestine missions into sensitive territories to provide air refueling for special operations aircraft. Secondary missions include air dropping special operations teams and other equipment as needed.

AFSOC COMMAND

PRIMARY SUBORDINATE UNITS

| AIR FORCE SPECIAL OPERATIONS FORCES (AFSOF) HURLBURT FLD, FL | 16 SOW HURLBURT FLD, FL | 193 SOW (ANG) HARRISBURG IAP, PA | USAFSOS HURLBURT FLD, FL | 353 SOG KADENA AB, JA | 352 SOG RAF MILDENHALL, UK | 18 FLTS HURLBURT FLD, FL | 720 STG HURLBURT FLD, FL | 919 SOW (AFRC) DUKE FLD, FL |

| ...S (PREDATOR) ...LBURT FLD, FL | 4 SOS (AC-130U) HURLBURT FLD, FL | 6 SOS (AVIATION FID, UH-1) HURLBURT FLD, FL | 8 SOS (MC-130E) DUKE FLD, FL | 9 SOS (MC-130E) EGLIN AFB, FL |

| ...SOS (MC-130H) ...LBURT FLD, FL | 16 SOS (AC-130H) HURLBURT FLD, FL | 19 SOS HURLBURT FLD, FL | 319 SOS (PC-12) HURLBURT FLD, FL | 20 SOS (MH-53J) HURLBURT FLD, FL |

| 22 STS McCHORD AFB, FL | 23 STS HURLBURT FLD, FL | 24 STS FT. BRAGG, NC |

| ...OS (MC-130H) ...MILDENHALL, UK | 21 SOS (MH-53J) RAF MILDENHALL, UK | 67 SOS (MC-130P) RAF MILDENHALL, UK | 321 STS RAF MILDENHALL, UK |

| 10 COMBAT WEATHER SQ HURLBURT FLD, FL | 21 STS POPE AFB, NC |

| 711TH SOS (MC-130E) DUKE FLD, FL | 5TH SOS)MC-130P) EGLIN AFB, FL |

| 1 SOS (MC-130H) KADENA AB, JA | 17 SOS (MC-130P) KADENA AB, JA | 320 STS KADENA AB, JA |

193rd Special Operations Group (Air National Guard)

Residing at Harrisburg International Airport, Pennsylvania, the 193rd is solely responsible for AFSOC's mission for providing airborne radio and television broadcasts. Flying the uniquely configured EC-130E Commando Solo aircraft, the unit can be deployed for PSYWAR operations during wartime or mobilized for humanitarian efforts in peacetime. Operating six of the Commando Solo aircraft, the 193rd can be deployed on a moment's notice around the globe. Anytime, anywhere.

123 Special Tactics Squadron (Air National Guard)

The 123 STS, based at Standiford Field, Kentucky, stands ready to deploy combat controllers and pararescuemen around the world in support of the Global War on Terrorism. The National Guard members of the 123 were deployed widely into both OEF and OIF theaters of operations.

Chapter 3

NEW MISSIONS

From early August 1990 to late February 1991, AFSOC participated in Operations Desert Shield and Desert Storm, the protection of Saudi Arabia, and liberation of Kuwait.

It was the Green Hornets Pave Lows of the 20th Special Operations Squadron that began the war in the Gulf. In October 1990, U.S. Commander in Chief Central Command (USCINCCENT) Gen. Norman H. Schwarzkopf had studied the multitude of maps, aerial and satellite imagery, and intelligence reports and pondered his next plan to action. It was the last week of the month when Col. Gary Gray of the 20th SOS met with the general. Colonel Gray briefed General Schwarzkopf on a plan called "Eager Anvil."

This plan intended for a flight of four MH-53 Pave Lows and an assault force of U.S. Army AH-64 Apache attack helicopters to execute the mission. The Pave Lows were equipped with FLIR, terrain avoidance radar, GPS, and other sophisticated electronics and navigational aids. They would cross into Iraq, leading the Apaches through the dark and over the featureless desert terrain to the target areas. Once on site the U.S. Army pilots in their Apaches would "take out" two enemy radar installations, simultaneously, with AGM-114 Hellfire laser-guided missiles. With these radar sites destroyed, a corridor opened for U.S. and Coalition aircraft to begin the air campaign.

So critical was this operation to the commencement of Desert Storm that General Schwarzkopf asked Colonel Gray, "Colonel, are you going to guarantee me one hundred percent success on this mission?" Colonel Gray looked at the general and answered, "Yes, sir." The USCINCCENT replied, "Then you get to start the war."

Lt. Col. Richard L. Comer was a little taken aback over Colonel Gray's commitment. Comer vowed that the mission would have to be perfect; he did not intend to make his boss a liar. He later commented, "This was the best joint helicopter flying operation I've ever seen." The Apaches were designed to shoot and destroy targets, and the Pave Lows were designed to get the AH-64s to the targets; it was a perfect match. The designation for the mission was Task Force Normandy. There were two formations of two MH-53Js and two AH-64s. One group was assigned to the eastern site, the other to the western-most installation.

AT 0212 TF Normandy crossed the border and entered Iraq. All of the training that the 20th had under their belts was now paying off. The helicopters sped through the pitch-black night flying no higher than 50 feet off the desert below. Relying on the Pave Lows' computers and sensors, the Green Hornets' pilots zigzagged around Nomad camps, down into wadis (a dry desert stream bed), flying NOE to stay under Iraqi radar. They staggered back and forth to avoid enemy observation posts.

The formations arrived on target, and at 0238 the sites were struck simultaneously by missiles. Within a span of four minutes, two Iraqi radar installations ceased to exist. The air campaign had begun. Another crucial mission conducted by AFSOC personnel was the placing of navigation beacons at various locations along the Saudi-Iraq borders. The STS teams working in conjunction with the 160 Special Operations Aviation Regiment (Airborne) carried out this task, which provided navigation guides for F-111 bombers going downtown (i.e., Baghdad).

Active-duty AFRES and ANG components of AFSOC were deployed to Saudi Arabia and Turkey: the 1st SOW with its AC-130s, HC-130s, MC-130s, MH-53s, and MH-60s; the 193rd SOG with its EC-130s; and the 919th SOG, with its AC-130s and HH-3s all deployed south of Kuwait.

Left: The special tactics squadron teams or STT are a combination of combat controllers, pararescuemen, and in some cases Special Operations weathermen. These battlefield airmen are the ground element of AFSOC, capable of being the "eyes and ears" of a theater commander. Here, members of the 23rd Special Tactics Squadron are armed with the Colt M4A1 and the M203, 40mm grenade launcher.

The 39th SOW deployed north of Iraq with its HC-130s, MC-130s, and MH-53s. Special tactics personnel operated throughout the theater on multiple combat control and combat rescue missions.

Air Force Specials Operation Command combat control teams were responsible for all air traffic control in the Persian Gulf theater of operations during Operation Desert Shield; once the war transitioned to Desert Storm this task was handed off to conventional ATC units. In addition to this, other missions performed were direct-action missions, combat search and rescue, infiltration, exfiltration, air base ground defense, air interdiction, special reconnaissance, close air support, psychological operations, and helicopter air refueling.

Post–Gulf War Events

Following the Gulf War, aircraft and personnel of the U.S. Air Force Special Operations Command stood alert for

This PJ walks point for his team, armed with a HK MP5, 9mm submachine-gun. The ever-watchful eyes of an STS team member provide cover for the team. Although the special tactics teams have transitioned to the M4A1 carbine, the MP-5 submachine-gun still can be found in the armories and may be used depending on the mission parameters.

personnel recovery and various other missions. In April 1991, Operation Provide Comfort provided humanitarian assistance in northern Iraq to Kurdish refugees after a revolt against the Iraqi government failed and more than a million Kurds fled into the mountains along the Turkey and Iranian borders. Additionally, Operation Southern Watch monitored the area of southern Iraq to ensure no incursion of Iraqi troops below the 32nd parallel. In July 1992, AFSOC units began participation in NATO Implementation Force (IFOR) operations in Bosnia.

Operation Provide Comfort gave humanitarian relief. During this operation more than fifteen tons of MREs were air-dropped. Operation Deny Flight enforced the no-fly zone and provided close air support to United Nations ground troops. In December 1992, AFSOC special tactics and intelligence personnel supported Operation Restore Hope in Somalia. In the spring of 1993, under Operation Continue Hope, humanitarian relief operations were secured with the help of AC-130H Spectre gunships. During this operation, special tactics team members would be operating with the Rangers from the 75th Ranger Regiment and Delta Force as part of Task Force Ranger.

The number of deployments following Operation Desert Storm was only exceeded by the number of organizational modifications. The more significant ones included the 353rd SOW relocation under Operation Fiery Vigil from Clark Air Base, Republic of Philippines, to Kadena Air Base, Japan, in June 1991 due to the volcanic eruption of Mount Pinatubo. The unit was supported by temporary duty personnel under Operation Scimitar Sweep for more than a year.

In January 1992, the 39th SOW relocated from Rhein-Main Air Base, Germany, to Royal Air Force Alconbury, United Kingdom, and later that year was inactivated and its personnel and equipment were reconstituted as the 352nd SOW. In December 1992, both overseas wings were redesignated as groups. During the summer of 1993 it was announced that the 352nd SOG would be moving again, this time to RAF Mildenhall.

More reorganization occurred on Hurlburt Field. The 1720th STGP became the 720th STG in March 1992. Ownership of Hurlburt Field was transferred from AMC to AFSOC in October 1992. This was followed by the merger of the 834th ABW into the 1st SOW, which assumed host unit responsibilities. A year later, the 1st SOW became the 16th SOW in a move to preserve U.S. Air Force heritage.

This Pave Low pilot from the 20th Special Operations Squadron (Green Hornets) wears his night-vision goggles in the down position, anticipating a mission to be executed under cover of darkness.

Chapter 4

GLOBAL WAR ON TERRORISM

After the terrorist attacks of September 11, 2001, the operational tempo of the U.S. military went through the roof and USSOCOM went into overdrive to ensure there were boots on the ground. Among those first units deployed in the Global War on Terrorism (GWOT) were members of the Air Force Special Operations Command. Special tactics team comprised of combat controllers, pararescuemen, and combat weathermen were positioned to establish air heads, helicopter landing zones, drops zones, close air support, and a plethora of other tasks for which these battlefield airmen were amply suited, trained, and capable.

Move…shoot…communicate. A team of a special tactics squadron with vehicles ready for action in Operation Enduring Freedom. The mission of the STS operators is to plan, prepare, and, when directed, integrate, synchronize, and control the elements of air and space power to execute air missions in support of America's Global War on Terrorism. *U.S. Air Force*

Left: On September 11, 2001, AFSOC was on the scene shortly after the attack had taken place. In the visor you can see the World Trade Center. Tower One has already fallen and Tower Two can still be seen reflected in the visor of an MH-53 helicopter crewmember. AFSOC Pave Lows responded immediately to support relief efforts in New York City and Washington, D.C. Since the Global War on Terrorism began, 16 SOW aircraft have flown more than eleven thousand combat sorties, amassing more than thirty-eight thousand combat hours. *U.S. Air Force*

Operation Enduring Freedom

The first assault launched by the United States in the Global War on Terrorism took place in October 2001. To make a statement, Rangers from the 75th Ranger Regiment performed an air drop into the Afghanistan night. This assault would launch the official start of America's response to the attacks the previous month. Prior to the deployment of the Rangers, a special operations weather team was on the ground. As the MC-130 Combat Talons, laden with Rangers headed for the drop zone, the combat weatherman reported on local conditions at the DZ.

An hour from the scheduled drop, reports arrived of heavy ground fog on the target. The call

Following the attack on America, one of the first U.S. Special Operations forces on the ground in Afghanistan was the special tactics teams. Here, combat controllers bring a C-17 transport into an undisclosed airfield during Operation Enduring Freedom. Their expertise in performing airfield surveys and assessments was invaluable in opening a functional airfield in the austere condition of the country. One combat controller remarked, "Anyone can land a plane once. The trick is having a usable runway and airfield." *U.S. Air Force*

came down from the commander to abort the drop. The combat weatherman on the ground radioed back in with the message, "Wait one. This will clear up in about fifteen minutes." With this information the Combat Talons maintained their heading to the DZ. As the SOWT had forecasted the fog lifted; the ramps lowered on the MC-130 aircraft and the Rangers exited the Talons dropping them on Objective Rhino; a Taliban compound located in Khandahar.

While Operation Rhino was taking place, Special Forces Operations detachments, or A-teams, were covertly inserted into Afghanistan by helicopters. The mission of these soldiers from the five Special Forces Group was to link up with the Northern Alliance forces and take the fight to the Taliban. Accompanying each of the ODAs was a combat controller whose mission was to provide close air support for the team.

Kabul

Flying in MH-53 Pave Lows, Operational Detachment Alpha 555, codename "Triple Nickel," was inserted into the Panjshir

Valley, north of Kabul. Its mission was to join Northern Alliance and liberate the Afghanistan capital city from the Taliban. Accompanying ODA-555 was Master Sgt. William Calvin Markham, a combat controller assigned to the 23rd special tactics squadron. The AFSOC NCO was armed with an M-4 rifle and an eighty-pound pack loaded with tools of the trade.

As the team inserted, they encountered numerous individuals closing on their position. The team went into a defense posture, yet did not engage. As it turned out, the men coming toward them in the darkness were indeed members of the Northern Alliance who greeted the Americans and welcomed them to their country and the fight. As they observed the Taliban lines, they would discover it was a sixty-kilometer front line, with guns, anti-aircraft-artillery, mortars, and tanks. The mission of ODA-555 would be to break through the Taliban lines and capture Kabul, the Afghanistan capital city.

With the U.S. SOF team on the ground, the tide of the war was about to take a giant turn in favor of the Northern

Alliance forces. The NA fighters would pick out a target and Master Sgt. Markham would mark it with the SOFLAM. A short time later a laser-guided bomb would fall from the sky and destroy the target. On one occasion the NA fighters pointed to a tank, which they had been trying to take out for three years. The combat controller identified the target, vectored in a fast mover, painted the target, and destroyed the tank all within twenty minutes. The NA forces were amazed at the accuracy of the laser-aiming device, so much that they seemed to avoid the device as if it was some type of death ray.

The accuracy of the attacks was not lost on the Taliban who began to mount a counterattack against the Northern Alliance and their newfound allies: Markham and ODA-555. On one side you had a handful of special operators, on the other side ten thousand Taliban fighters. The Taliban had a vast array of guns, tanks, and AAA as they dug in readying for a long fight.

However, what they did not know is there was now a combat controller on the ground, and for the next ten days he had at his disposal every aircraft that was in theater and even a few outside as well. The fighting continued for two weeks as the SOF operators worked around the clock as the U.S. Air Force pounded Kabul. The skies were filled with U.S. and British planes, from gunships to bombers, which rained death down on the enemy. All the time Master Sergeant Markham performed his mission with as much skill as a conductor directs his orchestra.

The fighting intensified and the Taliban mounted a counterattack, throwing everything at the American SOF team and the NA forces. Markham was pinned down, out manned, and out gunned. Training kicked in and he did what combat controllers do—shoot, move, and communicate. A B-52 bomber was on station and Markham called in an air strike, danger close.

At a classified airfield in Afghanistan, a ground mobility vehicle is loaded onto a MC-130P Combat Shadow. This scene would be repeated over and over as AFSOC aircrews inserted U.S. Special Operations forces through their area of operations as they hunted down Taliban and al-Qaeda fighters. Capable of landing in the dark, most likely the landing zone would already be marked out by a waiting special tactics team. *U.S. Air Force*

As the bombs fell, the NA commander shielded the body of the American. He would later explain, if he had died, his next in command would take over. If the American would die, the bombers would be gone. Master Sergeant Markham was awarded the Silver Star for his action in Kabul. Within the citation the U.S. Air Force credited Markham with, ". . . (D)irecting 175 sorties between Oct. 14 and Nov. 20 that resulted in eliminating 450 enemy vehicles and killing more than 3,500 Taliban fighters."

Intelligence had told the team they have six months to get into Kabul. With the precision-guided air strikes called in by Master Sergeant Markham and the tenacity of the Special Forces team, the mission was accomplished in twenty-five days. The AFSOC combat controller along with the SF ODA entered the U.S. Embassy in Kabul and raised the American flag over the site.

Fall of Mazar-e-Sharif

In November 2001, Operational Detachment Alpha (ODA) 595 from the U.S. Army's 5th Special Forces Group (Airborne) was working in northern Afghanistan with the warlord Abdul Rashid Dostum. Their mission was to combine

Master Sgt. Bart Decker, a combat controller from Air Force Special Operations Command at Hurlburt Field, Florida, rides on horseback with the Northern Alliance in Afghanistan. Gen. John P. Jumper, U.S. Air Force Chief of Staff, related, "Combat inspires the need to invent things on the spot when you have to handle difficult circumstances you've never come across before." Special Operations forces troops riding horse back in Afghanistan use laser devices to help relay target locations through laptops to a satellite as an example of how people handle difficult circumstances. *U.S. Air Force*

with ODA 534 who was working with Mohammed Atta and take down the Taliban fortress at Mazar-e-Sharif.

Assigned to the ODA was Master Sgt. Bart Decker a combat controller with the 720 Special Operations Group. Using various aircraft, Master Sergeant Decker was able to call in precision-guided munitions on the enemy forces. Due to the altitude of the B-52 bombers and F-16 aircraft, it was not unusually to "paint" the target and then wait approximately two minutes for the bomb to find its target. This amazed the commander of the Northern Alliance forces. He was able to see through the SOFLAM sight, yet saw no bombs, he heard the chirping of the laser designator, yet heard no aircraft. Then as if by magic, the target in front of him exploded. One ODA Captain related they thought the Americans processed a "death ray," so precise was the targeting.

This would be the first major factory for the Northern Alliance and was a significant defeat for the Taliban. Two ODAs, a couple of combat controllers, along with a handful of British SAS, and their Northern Alliance allies captured the Taliban fortress at Mazar-e-Sharif. These actions marked the collapse of the Taliban forces in northern Afghanistan, as thousands of Taliban and al-Qaeda fighters fled east to Kunduz in an assortment of pickups and FWD vehicles.

Khandahar

One of the largest helicopters assault since the Vietnam War would take place as U.S. Special Operations forces prepared to assault the compound of Taliban leader Mullah Mohammad Omar. A twelve-man special tactics team comprised of combat controllers, pararescuemen, and special operation weathermen were placed on the ground to perform a reconnaissance mission. Their RECCE (pronounced RECK-ee) mission was to provide detailed information on the helicopter landing zone, LHZ, and intelligence on enemy activity.

Tora Bora

The man to catch was Osama bin Laden; he had orchestrated the September 11 attacks on America. Intelligence had placed him in the Tora Bora region in what was a massive complex of caves and tunnels. Hearing this info the special operations dam broke; members of the Special Forces, Delta Force, and British SAS converged on the region to hunt down this elusive nomad referred to by his followers as "The Prince" or "The Director." Attached to these SOF units were members of AFSOC's special tactics squadron.

The combat controllers were responsible for bringing the fire power of U.S. and Coalition aircraft down to bear on the Taliban and al-Qaeda forces. During this operation in December 2001, combat controller Technical Sergeant "Mike" worked constantly calling in multiple CAS missions on the enemy. His use of radio, GPS, and laser targeting systems allowed him to place munitions with surgical accuracy and volume unprecedented prior to the attack on Tora Bora.

During the heat of the battle, Technical Sergeant Mike moved from the relative safety of his position forward to assist the local Afghan fighters in their assault against the enemy. All the while he was coming under heavy machinegun and mortar fire. He controlled more than three hundred CAS storied from multiple aircraft, ranging from AV-8B Harrier to B-52 bombers; as well as expended the full combat loads of five AC-130 gunships. Overall, when the dust had settled, he had personally directed more than 600,000 pounds of ordinance on enemy targets. Yet, in spite of all this destructive power, as the SOF units tightened their hold on the region, it

Seen here is one of the many bunkers used by the Taliban and al-Qaeda forces. From the air, the bunkers are almost invisible as they blend in with the terrain. This is a case where intelligence and photos from an orbiting UAV was not enough; you had to have boots on the ground and eyes on the target. During the battle of Tora Bora, one combat controller personally called in more than six hundred thousand pounds of ordnance with pinpoint accuracy on enemy positions. *U.S. Air Force*

was like tightening your grip on a handful of sand, and Osama bin Laden slipped through the gaps.

Operation Anaconda-Takur Ghar

In March 2002 U.S. and coalition forces commenced Operation Anaconda in the mountainous region near the Shah-e-Kot Valley. Operation Anaconda was part of the ongoing effort in Afghanistan to root out Taliban and al-Qaeda forces holed up in the Pakitia Province area of the country. The operation began March 3 with the insertion of U.S. and coalition forces into the region south of Kabul. What made Takur Ghar so important to Operation Anaconda was it had a commanding view of the entire valley from the mountaintop. Unfortunately, military positions are a lot like real estate, and if you think someplace is great to set up an OP, chances are the enemy has the same thoughts.

Such was the case in the early hours of 4 March 2002 when an MH-47E of the 2nd Battalion, 160 Special Operations Aviation Regiment, call sign "Razor O3," attempted to insert a team of U.S. Navy SEALs and an AFSOC combat controller, Technical Sgt. John Chapman, onto the mountaintop and came under heavy machinegun and RPG fire. Evading the ground fire, the pilot immediately pulled pitch, and despite an RPG hit to the hydraulics, managed to extract the helicopter out of harm's way, setting the damaged aircraft down seven kilometers away. Unbeknownst to him at the time was one of the SEALs, Petty Officer 1st Class Neil Roberts, fell from the helicopter, landing in the snow-covered mountain some ten feet below.

Knowing that PO1C Roberts was all alone on the HLZ, Technical Sergeant Chapman quickly established radio contact with an AC-130 gunship. The gunship provided protection for the downed aircraft and team. Once the area was secure, Chapman directed the gunship to initiate a search for the lone SEAL. Using the aircraft's sophisticated sensors, the aircrew begin looking for Roberts; additionally, a Predator UAV was also in position overhead.

At Chapman's request and direction, another 160 Chinook, "Razor 04," extracted the SOF team and crew from the downed helicopter. The special operations team was ready to return to the mountaintop in an attempt to rescue Roberts. The combat controller jumped on the aircraft to assist in the rescue attempt. As the MH-47E inserted the team it came under heavy machinegun and RPG fire. Chapman was the first man down the ramp and immediately engaged two Taliban fighters. Under fire and with minimal cover, he continued forward, concentrating his fire on an enemy machinegun nest. He continued to attack the enemy until he was mortally wounded. Technical Sergeant Chapman would become the first combat controller killed in action since the Vietnam War. His quick and decisive action against the enemy forces gave the remaining team members the time they needed to get to defensive positions. The SEAL team leader of the rescue related that Chapman's actions had undeniably saved the entire rescue team.

However, the team was not out of the woods, surrounded by Taliban and al-Qaeda fighters, the rescuers had now become in need of rescuing themselves.

The quick reaction force was ordered to the mountaintop where they were to rescue the entrapped operators and destroy the enemy. The two helicopters carrying the QRF were "Razor 01" and "Razor 02." Aboard the lead Chinook were ten members of the 75th Ranger Regiment; an ETAC airman; U.S. Air Force combat controller Staff Sgt. Gabe Brown, 22nd special tactics squadron; along with Senior Airman Jason Cunningham, 38th Rescue Squadron, and Techical Sgt. Keary Miller, 123rd Special Tactics Squadron, both AFSOC pararescuemen. As the MH-47 helicopter came in from the south, "Razor 01" was hit on the starboard side by a RPG and

Takur Ghar, or Roberts Ridge as it would be called, was a very costly piece of real estate in the Afghan mountains. A total of eight U.S. SOF operators would be killed in action before the fight was over. Seen here is what is left of an MH-47E helicopter of the 160th Special Operations Aviation Regiment. The helicopter, "Razor 01," had been so severely damaged during the assault on the mountain it was unable to be removed from the site. The wreckage was left on the mountain and a U.S. air strike was called in to destroy the aircraft. *U.S. Air Force*

it came under intense ground fire from three other directions by machineguns and small arms fire. Try as they might to abort the landing, the Chinook was too severely damaged to fly and dropped to the mountain some ten feet below.

As the battle raged around the disabled aircraft, combat controller, Staff Sgt. Brown called in and directed CAS for the next fifteen hours. With enemy fighters as close as 20 meters away, the combat controller was often calling the air strikes "danger close." His actions would turn the tide in favor of the SOF units on the snow-covered top of Takur Ghar. As the day of fighting came to a close, seven courageous SOF troops had made the ultimate sacrifice; among them two AFSOC special tactics airmen, Technical Sgt. John Chapman and Senior Airman Jason Cunningham. Not since Task Force

The special tactics teams work closely with the U.S. Army Special Forces. Here, a combat controller prepares to search a cave along with an SF ODA member in the mountainous terrain of Afghanistan. These battlefield airmen provide an extra layer of lethality operating with any of the SOF units. Both operators are armed with M4A1 carbines equipped with various SOPMOD accessories. *U.S. Air Force*

Positioned among the scrub brush in the Afghanistan mountains, a combat controller prepares for his next fire mission. Using the laser designator, he will be able to place a laser-guide smart bomb accurately on target. The placement of a combat controller on the ground and a fast mover or gunship overhead results in one of the most lethal weapon combinations in the U.S. arsenal. *U.S. Air Force*

Ranger in Mogadishu, Somalia, in October 1993 had the SOF community experienced such an intense firefight as in the battle for Roberts Ridge, named after the fist man to fall, PO1C Neil Roberts.

Since the first battlefield airman was inserted into Afghanistan in support of OEF until today, numerous missions have been carried out by these twenty-first-century Air Commandos. Missions such as that of Technical Sgt. Bradley Reilly, a combat controller with the 23rd Special Tactics Squadron, Hurlburt Field, Florida, continue to be conducted every day in support of OEF/OIF. Technical Sergeant Reilly was serving on the Quick Reaction Force as the joint terminal attack controller assigned to Special Forces ODA 163, call sign "The Beast." After answering a call from an allied general, the QRF aboard two Black Hawks were returning to the FOB. En route they observed anti-collation militia, ACM, and set down to investigate.

At first there was sporadic gunfire, which then erupted into several ACM fighters engaging Technical Sergeant Bradley and the SF soldier with him. The gunfire had wounded both of the men, yet in spite of his wounds, Technical Sergeant Bradley continued to engage the enemy with his M4A1 carbine. He tended to the wounded "green beret" and called in AH-64 Apache gunships and A-10 Warthogs, which had been on station. As the result of his actions, the enemy was eliminated, the SF soldier survived, and Technical Sergeant Bradley would be awarded the Silver Star and Purple Heart medals for his decisive actions on that Afghanistan mountainside.

During a visit to the Combat Control School at Pope AFB, Defense Secretary Donald H. Rumsfeld commented that "Some 85 percent of the air strikes in Operation Enduring Freedom were called in by U.S. Air Force combat controllers."

Operation Iraqi Freedom

Maj. Gen. Stanley McChrystal, U.S. Army vice chief of operations on the Joint Staff stated, "Operation Iraqi Freedom is supported by the largest special operations force since the Vietnam War." Many of the missions conducted by AFSOC during OIF remain classified; however, a few have begun to come to light. AFSOC three MC-130 from the 919 SOW refueled half a dozen MH-53 Pave Lows serving as infiltration platform for SOF units as well as "other government agency" personnel.

Even though they lost one Pave Low, the Air Commandos drove on and carried out their mission eight hours before the forty-eight-hour deadline President George W. Bush gave Saddam Hussein. Mere hours before the collation aircraft released the Shock and Awe of OIF, the 919 SOW using MC-130E Combat Talons inserted a hundred SOF personnel, including vehicles and more than 119,000 pounds of gear, into Wadi al Kir airfield in Iraq. AFSOC personnel would be infiltrated along with their equipment to establish airfields for follow forces.

Members of the 123rd special tactics squadron, an Air National Guard component of AFSOC, was instrumental in successful operations in northern Iraq. As part of Task

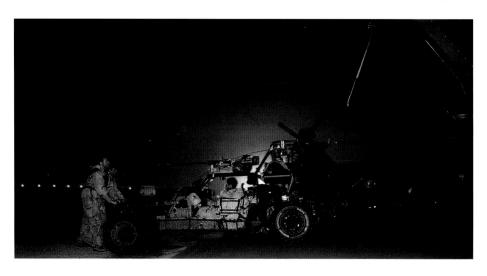

A SEAL desert patrol vehicle is loaded onto an MH-53 in preparation for their next mission. Whether it be direct action, special reconnaissance, or other tasks, the Pave Low crew will get them on target and on time. *U.S. Air Force*

Force Viking, the ST teams were inserted into Iraq covertly via MC-130. Once on the ground they worked with SF ODAs in training Kurdish fighters in the forward non-permissive region. Their mission was to establish and train two militias: the Kurdish Democratic Part (KDP), consisting of approximately forty thousand fighters, and the Party for a Unified Kurdistan (PUK), numbering around twenty thousand troops.

Combat controllers in another region operating with SF ODAs engaged Republican Guard north of Karbala. The urban environment had turned to a sea of green as Iraqi soldiers appeared in every window, doorway, and rooftop. As bullets rained down on the U.S. SOF teams, the combat controller radioed in close air support. A pair of A-10 Warthogs orbiting in the area answered the call for CAS. The area was heavily populated and there was a concern regarding collateral damager, so they could not release their bombs. Instead the pilots came in with their 30mm cannons blazing and routed the Iraqi soldiers.

Above: Members of the special tactics teams integrate seamlessly with other SOF units. The STT complements the unit by bringing a vast array of warfighting skills (i.e., austere airfield control, terminal attack control, personnel rescue and recovery, assault zone assessment, battlefield trauma care, and combat weather forecasting). Note the desert "tiger stripe" BDUs as well as the assortment of SOPMOD accessories. *U.S. Air Force*

Operating in northern Iraq, the members of the special tactics teams provide support to the Kurds as well as U.S. Special Operations forces. This Kurdish fighter is armed with an M240, while the U.S. operator carries an AK47 variant. The STT provides close air support, command, and control as well as interfacing with UAVs to determine enemy location, composition, and strength. *U.S. Air Force*

Western Iraq

Special Operations forces were also responsible for attacking a number of specific targets such as airfields, weapons of mass destruction sites, and command and control headquarters. In the West, one of the crucial tasks for the SOF units was a large area denial mission. On 14 March 2003, five days before the official start of Operation Iraqi Freedom, the morning quiet was turned into deafening explosions. The source of the attack came from a pair of B-1Bs from an undisclosed location somewhere in southwest Asia from an attack and airfield complex 250 miles west of Baghdad. The complex, known merely as H3 Al Walid airbase, would serve as a staging point for Delta, SAS, 45 Commando, and Australian SASR. Supported by AFSOC forces, this who's who list of SOF units carry out a variety of missions, including "Scud Hunting."

Additionally, H1 and H2 airbases were seized by the 75th Ranger Regiment on the night of 25 March 2003. Supporting the seizures of these strategic objectives were the MH-53 Pave Lows, AC-130 gunships, and special tactics teams. The significance of these bases was their close proximity to the Jordanian border. From here U.S. and allied special operations team maneuvered eastward toward Baghdad. While they traverse across the desert, AFSOC UAVs are overhead providing reconnaissance for their route of travel.

A special tactics team prepares their equipment prior to a mission in support of Operation Iraqi Freedom. Depending on the mission, the team will carry an assortment of gear that may include: UHF/VHF radio, intra-team radio, headsets, GPS units, SOFLAM, laser ranger finder, laser pointers, scopes, thermal video, beacons, tactical UAV, Panasonic "Toughbook" computer, extra batteries, food, water, ammunition along with primary and secondary weapons. When you add it up, the total weight of the equipment will often exceed that of the operator. *U.S. Air Force*

Battle of Debecka Pass

On 26 March 2003, Special Forces ODA 391 and 392 off loaded their ground mobility vehicles from an MC-130 Combat Talon in northern Iraq. They would link up with ODA 044 and their Kurdish Peshmerga fighters (translated to "Not afraid to die"); attached to the ODAs were combat controllers. There mission codename Northern Safari was to secure critical intersection located in the vicinity of Debecka between Irbil and Kirkuk. Their orders were to hold until relieved by elements of the 173rd Airborne.

Just after midnight on 6 April 2003, B-52s bombed the ridgeline between the SOF teams and the objective.

As the U.S. and their allies closed in on the city, they were engaged by Iraqi forces. While the SF soldiers engaged the enemy with .50-caliber machineguns and Javelin shoulder launched missiles, combat controllers called in close air support. During the firefight, the SF and CCTs had successfully engaged an Iraqi infantry brigade reinforced with T-55 tanks and MTLB armored personnel carries, without a single American casualty.

Mukarayin Dam

As U.S. and coalition forces pressed their attack on Baghdad in April 2003, military planners became concerned about the Mukarayin Dam located 57 miles northeast of the Iraqi capital. Though there was no military activity at or near the hydro-electric dam, it did offer the enemy a tempting target. Should the Iraqis decide to blow up the dam, it would send waves of water surging down on Baghdad, flooding the city. It was decided that a combined team of U.S. Navy SEALs along with Polish Grom commandos would secure the dam.

Providing the insertion platform for the commandos would be the 20th Special Operations Squadron. For several days the SEAL/Grom teams practiced their assault tactics, techniques, and procedures. When the time came, they loaded onto several Pave Low helicopters and began their insertion

A special tactics team conducts a check of a hanger at Baghdad International Airport in Iraq. The STT are often the first SOF operators on the ground to ensure the airfield is capable of sustaining follow-on aircraft. The members of AFSOC bring an essential skill set to the SOF in the Global War on Terrorism. *U.S. Air Force*

from their base in Kuwait. Crammed inside the helicopters, the teams traveled for five hours under a moonless night, including the aerial refueling of each of the aircraft by a KC-130 tanker.

When they reached their target, the pilots of the MH-53 helicopters had to avoid several high-voltage power lines as they hovered over the dam. The crew members deployed the thick nylon ropes and the commandos quickly fast roped to the ground. Once down, they raced to their prearranged sites on the dam, adjacent power station, and several surrounding buildings. The securing of the site proved to be one of the final missions carried out during the major combat phases of Operation Iraqi Freedom.

Predators

Members of AFSOC are responsible for running the unmanned aerial vehicles, UAVs in Operation Iraqi Freedom.

They can be found working with the Kurds and Special Forces in the north, running surveillance missions in Baghdad, and just about anywhere in between.

On one mission the Predator teams were providing over watch along the Euphrates River. On several occasions U.S. and coalition forces had come under machinegun fire. Utilizing the UAV, the AFSOC pilots switched over to thermal imaging and discovered Iraqi insurgents hiding on barges on the river. The UAVs were also instrumental in SOF infiltration and exfiltration. In one case it was discovered that an SOF infiltration landing zone (LZ) had been compromised and with the new information the team executed a real-time divert to a new LZ (surveyed by the same Predator) and ensuring the safe accomplishment of the mission.

The UAVs allowed the U.S. Air Force to be the hammer to the ground forces anvil. As the ground component marched toward Baghdad, the Predators provided crucial

A team of pararescuemen practice first-aid techniques during a training exercise at Baghdad International Airport during Operation Iraqi Freedom. While PJs are among the foremost medical specialists in the military, they remain "shooters" and are as skilled with weapons as they are with IVs and stethoscopes. *U.S. Air Force*

real-time targeting data to air and ground commanders, allowing Coalition Air Forces to destroy substantial enemy units in the path of U.S. ground forces, ensuring a swift march to the capital.

Lt. Gen. Walter E. Buchanan III, the Commander of U.S. Central Command Air forces, related to the House Armed Services Committee in the U.S. Congress, "Our UAVs leveraged the ability of other air force assets to attack key Iraqi command and control facilities and leadership targets. We were simultaneously destroying fielded forces, command and control centers, supporting our Special Operations forces, and ensuring that we gained and maintained air superiority and supremacy. We were successful in meeting and surpassing our goals, and twenty-one days later Baghdad fell into Coalition hands."

The commander of Air Force Special Operations Command, Lieutenant General Michael W. Wooley, related combat controllers who used small Bat-Cam unmanned aerial vehicles that weighed as little as two pounds and could be carried in the airman rucksack. These small UAVs extended the situational awareness of the battlefield airman up to three miles. This intelligence allowed the combat controllers to call in air strikes on insurgent concentrations along the SOF team's route of travel far enough in advance to remove the threat before a ground firefight occured. From 20 March 2003 when coalition forces invaded Iraq and concluding 1 May 2003, not a single SOF unit operating in OIF with an AFSOC combat controller equipped with a small UAV was ambushed by enemy forces.

The AFSOC air crews above and the special tactics squadrons on the ground continue to carry out a variety of missions as America continues to prosecute the Global War on Terrorism. It may be providing CAS or the covert insertion of an SOF unit. Whether it is a lone battlefield airman attached to an ODA, an STT inserted to establish an air head for follow-on forces, or the aircrews, the men and women of the U.S. Air Force Special Operations Command continue to bring a lethality of force to any mission. As in the past, today they remain an integral part of a huge percentage of U.S. military combat missions around the globe.

Chapter 5

SPECIAL OPERATIONS AIRCRAFT

The backbone of the Special Operations Wings is the venerable Lockheed C-130s. With more than forty years under its wings, the Hercules has more than lived up to its name. Its origins date back to the mid-fifties when the U.S. Air Force was looking for a turboprop transport to be used by the Military Airlift Transport Service (MATS), later known as Military Airlift Command (MAC) and the Tactical Air Command (TAC). The first production C-130, often called the "Herky-Bird," made its first flight on 7 April 1955. The initial deployment went to the Tactical Air Command in December 1956. The Hercules set an entirely new standard in tactical airlift. Through the years the C-130 has been in service in more than twenty countries and has evolved into many variants, four of which are important to special operations.

Tracing its heritage back to Vietnam, "Puff the Magic Dragon," "Spooky," "Stinger," and "Spectre" were names that brought fear into the hearts of the enemy forces and, more

The primary missions of the AC-130U gunship are close air support, air interdiction, and force protection. Close air support missions are in support of troops in contact with enemy forces, convoy escort, and operations. Air interdiction missions are conducted against preplanned targets or targets of opportunity. Force protection missions include air base defense and facilities defense. The call sign for the U-model gunship is "Spooky"; while the H model is called "Spectre."

Left: The current flagship of AFSOC is the AC-130U model "Spooky." So intricate is the weapons system, the AC-130U has a more complex wiring system than the NASA space shuttle. This particular aircraft is in operations with the 4th Special Operations Squadron at Hurlburt Field, Florida. From Roberts Ridge to Tora Bora and hundreds of other sorties, the AC-130 gunship brings a devastating lethality to the battlefield.

often than can be covered here, the relief and accolades of U.S. troops, both Special Forces and conventional. From its origin of the AC-47 with multiple miniguns through today, the gunship has evolved into a sophisticated, highly technical aircraft capable of turning the night sky into death. During Operation Restore Democracy in Haiti, Lt. Col. Tim Schaffer of the 4th Special Operations Squadron reported that AFSOC put the AC-130 gunships on station even though there was no hostile activity. "It gave the troops on the ground peace of mind to hear the drone of those engines overhead, just in case."

AC-130U "Spooky" Gunship

The newest of the AC-130 gunships and the current "flagship" of the Air Commando skies is the AC-130U. At a value of $190 million, this new Spooky was built with special operations in mind. Its primary mission is to deliver precision firepower in support of close air support for special operations and conventional ground forces. Close air support (CAS) is defined as air action against hostile targets that are in close proximity to friendly forces and require detailed integration of each air mission with the fire and movement of those forces. The Spooky can provide accurate fire support with limited collateral damage and can remain on station for extended periods of time. These activities are primarily performed in the cloak of darkness.

The business end of the gunship is found in three weapon systems. As you enter the AC-130U by way of the front crew hatch and turn to your right, you'll find the first

The AC-130U operates with a crew of thirteen. The gunship is armed with a 25mm Gatling gun, 40mm cannon, and a 105mm cannon. The "Spooky" gunship has a longer loiter time than the fast movers and can deliver highly accurate placement of low-yield munitions, desirable in CAS missions. Additionally, the AC-130U is equipped with a high-resolution sensor and enhanced communications suite compared to the tactical jet aircraft. While still in evaluation, future versions of the gunship may see a stealthier aircraft with the incorporation of missiles and laser systems. *U.S. Air Force*

weapon system, the GAU-12/U 25mm Gatling gun, which is fully traversable and is also capable of firing 1,800 rounds per minute from altitudes of up to twelve thousand feet. The 25mm weapon system automatically ejects the spent brass into a holding area where it is emptied out at a later time. There is no longer a need for the crew to shovel out the shell casings after a mission. This feature provides a safer environment for the crew as they will not trip over loose 25mm shells on the fuselage floor. Munitions available for the GAU-12 include the PGU-25 and PGU-38 high-explosive incendiary (HEI) and PGU-23 target practice (TP) round. The PGU-25 and PGU-38 HEI are effective against exposed personnel and light materials with both fragmentation and incendiary effects. The PGU-23 TP is primarily used for target practice, although it does provide some penetration capability. The TP round is most effective when mixed with HEI to provide an impact signature.

Two holdovers from the A and H model gunships are the 40mm Bofors guns and the 105mm Howitzer cannon—both battle-tested weapons. The 40mm Bofors gun has been associated with the gunships since 1969. Once used on naval vessels as anti-aircraft guns, the weapons were stripped down from pedestal mounts and placed in the AC-130s. The 40mm Bofors is mounted in the port side of the AC-130U with the ammunition stored in a special rack on the starboard wall of the fuselage, behind the gun.

Ammunition for the 40mm Bofors includes a variety of projectiles. The primary ordnance is the PGU-9B/B and PGU-9C/B high explosive incendiary (HEI) Zirconium liner cartridges. Other cartridges include the PGU-9B HEI-P Misch metal liner, the MK-2 series HE-P and HEI-P cartridges (primarily used for training), and the M81 series armor piercing (AP) projectile, some of which contain twelve-second-burn-time tracer elements (approximately ten thousand feet). The PGU-9B/B and PGU-9C/B HEI rounds are very effective against personnel, light vehicles, and as an incendiary for open flammables. The PRU-9B is a little less effective against the same target, as it contains less HE filler, resulting in a less effective fragmentation. The 40mm is preferred for CAS in "danger close" support to friendly forces due to its small fragmentation pattern.

The port side of an AC-130U gunship in operation with the 4th Special Operations Squadron. From this angle, the weapon systems are clearly visible. Located just aft of the crew door is the 25mm minigun. Moving toward the rear past the landing gear is the 40mm BFORS and then the 105mm Howitzer cannon. Continuing up the fuselage toward the tail is the direct infrared counter measure (DIRCM).

An up-close-and-personal view of the GAU-12/U 25mm General Electric Gatling gun. An upgrade from the 20mm gun, this new 25mm is traversable. The crew no longer has to shovel spent brass after a fire mission. The unit will automatically dispose of the cartridges for later removal. No more tripping on shell casings.

The other veteran on board, just aft of the Bofors, is the M102, 105mm Howitzer cannon. This weapon was derived from the U.S. Army field artillery M1A1 Howitzer. It has been modified to fire from an aircraft and is placed in a special mounting and positioned in the port side of the gunship. The M102 fires both the M1, 32.5-pound high explosive (HE), and the M60, 34.2-pound white phosphorous (WP) projectile at a range of 11,500 meters. The fuses for the HE rounds are super-quick M557, selectable to point detonation or a 0.05-second time delay; the hard-end FMU-153B with point detonation or 0.004- to 0.009-second delay; and the M732 proximity fuse, which detonates approximately seven meters above the ground or point detonation if not set for delay. The M1 HE projectiles with fast-fuse point detonation are effective against personnel and light vehicles. While the HE round with fuse delay is effective against light structures and personnel under heavy cover or foliage, the HE FMU-153B would be used for hardened target penetration capability. The M60 WP round, used only with the M557 fuse, is an effective smoke round with limited incendiary effect.

Unlike higher-speed fixed-wing aircraft (a.k.a., "fast movers"), which must have qualified forward air controllers (FACs) for ord-

As lethal as the AC-130U can be, the loitering flight during its firing pattern makes it vulnerable to surface-to-air missile attacks. To defend the aircraft and crew, "Spooky" has been fitted with the direct infrared counter measure (DIRCM) anti-missile system, which can be seen attached to both sides of the fuselage. Also of note are the electronic counter measures (ECM) in the modified beavertail of the aircraft.

A closer look at the horizon indicator on the instrument cluster indicates the gunship is in a port-side pylon turn. The AC-130U will perform a banking maneuver so its weapons may be unleashed upon the designated targets.

nance delivery in close position to friendly forces, the AC-130U can be controlled by fire support officers, team leaders, or self-FAC. This unique capability makes the gunship user-friendly for the operators on the ground, but requires a high degree of flexibility on the part of its crew.

These fire-control officers are located onboard the gunship in the battle management center (BMC). Here they operate the state-of-the-art sensors, navigation, and fire-control systems in a work area protected by a composite armor of silicon carbide and Spectra fiber. The BMC, coupled with the trained eyes and skilled hands of its officers, enables the crew to deliver the Spooky's firepower or area saturation with surgical precision. This is accomplished even in adverse weather conditions and total darkness.

The assortment of sensors fitted in this modern gunship consist of an all-light level television (ALLTV) system, a laser illuminator assembly (LIA), and an infrared detection set. A multimode radar furnishes exceptionally long-range target direction and identification. This radar is also able to track 40mm and 105mm projectiles and return pinpoint impact locations to the crew for subsequent target adjustment.

The fire-control systems offer a dual-target attack capability. Engaging two different sensors and using both weapons, the 40mm Bofors cannon and 105mm Howitzer have been updated with improved electronics that allow simultaneous aiming at two separate targets by the gunnery crew. As long as the two targets are within a mile of each other, the gunship can divide its fire with devastating accuracy. No other air-to-ground attack platform in the world offers this capability.

The new AC-130U is fully pressurized, allowing greater speeds, increased range, and additional crew comfort due to its ability to fly above, rather than through, adverse weather. Navigational features include inertial navigation systems (INS) and the GPS. The U-model gunship is capable of operation in adverse weather, in poor visibility, using the APQ180 strike radar. The radar will track fixed or moving targets or beacon offsets.

Defensive systems include a countermeasures dispensing system that releases chaff and flares to counter radar and infrared-guided anti-aircraft missiles. To shield the aircraft's heat signature from the engines, the AC-130 U has infrared heat shields mounted underneath the engines to dispense and hide the engine's heat source from hostile anti-aircraft with counter-IR devices with the introduction of the directional infrared countermeasures system, or DIRCM. DIRCM fires a laser at incoming heat-seeking missiles, blinding their optics and ruining their ability to track the aircraft, causing it to miss.

While close air support is the Spooky's primary mission, additional tasks it may undertake include air interdiction, armed reconnaissance, airbase, perimeter, and point defense; land, water, and heliborne troop escort; drop, landing, and extraction zone support; forward air control; limited airborne command and control; and combat search and rescue support.

At the conclusion of extensive testing by the U.S. Air Force Flight Test Center, the U-model Spooky was delivered to AFSOC on 1 July 1994. Thirteen of these aircraft are now assigned to the 16th Special Operations Wing's 4th Special Operations Squadron.

The AC-130 gunships were among the first AFSOC aircraft deployed to support Operations Enduring Freedom and Iraqi Freedom. Having the ability to loiter over the area of operations, the gunships were used as a force multiplier by providing precision close air support.

As the AC-130U Spooky flies into the twenty-first century, there are developmental plans being evaluated to make the gunship even more lethal. The current 25mm Gatling gun and the 40mm Bofors gun will be replaced with two 30mm Mark 44 Bushmaster II canons. In addition to the weapons upgrades AFSOC is testing the Viper Strike laser guided precision munitions. Manufactured by Northrop Grumman Corporation, the Viper Strike uses a combination of laser guidance and GPS to hone in on its target. The system would allow the AC-130 gunships to engage the enemy from higher altitude and a great standoff distance. Currently in evaluation, if approved, it could be in AFSOC gunships by 2010.

AC-130U Specifications

Contractor: Boeing; **powerplant:** four Allison T56-A15 turboprop engines; **thrust:** 4,910 equivalent shaft power; **wingspan:** 132 feet, 7 inches (40.4 meters); **length:** 97 feet, 9 inches (29.8 meters); **height:** 38 feet, 6 inches (11.7 meters); **speed:** 300 miles per hour (at sea level); **range:** approximately 2,200 nautical miles, unlimited with air refueling; **ceiling:** 30,000 feet; **maximum takeoff weight:** 155,000 pounds (69,750 kilograms, peacetime), 175,000 pounds (wartime); **armament:** one GAU-12/U 25mm General Electric Gatling

gun (firing rate of 3,600 rounds per minute; with a maximum of 4,200 RPM), one L-60 40mm Bofors cannon (firing rate of 100 shots per minute), one M-102 105mm cannon (firing rate of 6 to 10 rounds per minute); **avionics:** Hughes APG-80 fire-control radar, Texas Instruments AN/AAQ-117 forward looking infrared (FLIR) for 180 degree IR scanning, Gec-Marconi all-active, low-light level television (AALLLTV), INS/GPS navigation, ALQ-172 RF electronic countermeasures system, and ALR-69 radar warning receiver; **crew:** 13 total—five officers (pilot, copilot, navigator, fire-control officer, and electronic warfare [EW] officer) and eight enlisted (flight engineer, AALLTV operator, IR detection operator, four gunners, and loadmaster).

AC-130H "Spectre" Gunship

The predecessor to the U-model, the H-model Spectre gunship, armed with 20-, 40-, and 105mm cannons, can deliver precision firepower in support of close air support missions. This includes alternate missions: air interdiction; armed reconnaissance; airbase, perimeter, and point defense; land, water, and heliborne troop escort; drop, landing, and extraction zone support; forward air control; limited airborne command and control; and CSAR support.

Heavily armed, the AC-130H incorporates side-firing weapons integrated with sophisticated sensor, navigation, and fire-control systems to provide surgical firepower or area saturation during extended periods, primarily at night as well as in inclement weather.

Included in the sensor array are lowlight television (LLTV) and infrared (IR) sensors. The H-model is also equipped with radar and electronic devices that give the gunship a positive IFF (identify friend/foe) to distinguish between supporting friendly ground forces and efficient delivery of ordnance on hostiles during all weather conditions. Navigation devices include an inertial navigation system and GPS.

During Operation Desert Storm, the Spectres provided air base defense and close air support for ground forces. While AFSOC aircraft and squadrons would play a primary role, it would not be without a high cost. AFSOC suffered its only loss of the war, an AC-130H of the 16th Special Operations Squadron—"Spirit 03" and a crew of 14. This was the single largest "air" loss during the Persian Gulf War. Again, the men of AFSOC would live up to the heritage of the Air Commandos and make the ultimate sacrifice for their country and freedom.

Subsequently, the AC-130s were also used in Operation Continue Hope and United Shield in Somalia. In addition, Spectre gunships played a pivotal role in support of IFOR missions in Bosnia-Herzegovina. As NATO launched a three-day assault on Bosnian Serb targets, AC-130H gunships were tasked with targeting and destroying artillery and radar sites positioned around Sarajevo.

AC-130H Specifications

Contractor: Lockheed; **powerplant:** four Allison turboprop engines T56-A15; **thrust:** 4,910 equivalent shaft power; **wingspan:** 132 feet, 7 inches (40.4 meters); **length:** 97 feet, 9 inches (29.8 meters); **height:** 38 feet, 6 inches (11.7 meters); **speed:** 300 miles per hour (at sea level); **range:** approximately 2,200 nautical miles, unlimited with air refueling; **ceiling:** 30,000 feet; **maximum takeoff weight:** 155,000 pounds (69,750 kilograms, peacetime), 175,000 pounds (wartime); **armament:** two 20mm Vulcan cannons with 3,000 rounds, one 40mm Bofors cannon with 256 rounds, and one 105mm Howitzer with 100 rounds; **crew:** 14 total—five officers (pilot, copilot, navigator, fire-control officer, and electronic warfare [EW] officer) and nine enlisted (flight engineer, LLTV operator, IR detection operator, five gunners, and loadmaster).

MC-130E/H Combat Talon

The MC-130E Combat Talon I and the MC-130H Combat Talon II are designed for long-range clandestine or covert delivery of Special Operations forces and equipment and to provide global, day, night, and adverse weather capability to air-drop and air-land personnel and equipment in support of U.S. and allied Special Operations forces.

Combat Talons are equipped with FLIR, terrain following/avoidance radars, and specialized aerial delivery equipment. Incorporated into the Talons are a fully integrated inertial navigation (IIN), GPS, and a high-speed aerial delivery system. These special systems are used to locate small drop zones and deliver personnel or equipment with greater accuracy and at higher speeds than possible with a "vanilla" C-130. Such an example is U.S. Army Special Forces (Green Berets) or U.S. Navy SEALs operating in a sensitive or hostile territory.

A MC-130H Combat Talon II of the 15th SOS on the tarmac at Hurlburt Field. In order to keep the avionics cool while running on the ground, an air-conditioning unit is attached to the aircraft.

An MC-130H Combat Talon lands at an undisclosed airstrip in Afghanistan. The mission of the MC-130E Combat Talon I and MC-130H Combat Talon II is to provide global, day, night, and adverse weather capability to air-drop as well as air-land personnel and equipment. Capable of flying as low as two hundred fifty feet, these aircraft are equipped with in-flight refueling equipment; terrain-following, terrain-avoidance radar; an inertial and global positioning satellite navigation system; and a high-speed aerial delivery system. The aircraft is able to penetrate hostile airspace at low altitudes and crews are specially trained in night and adverse weather operations.
U.S. Air Force

An MC-130H Combat Talon II comes in for a landing at Hurlburt Field. Encased in the large nose is the AN/APQ-170 multi-mode radar (MMR). Directly beneath can be seen the forward looking infrared (FLIR) allowing the Talon to penetrate hostile airspace. This Talon has been modified giving the aircraft the capability to conduct aerial refueling operations. The outermost pylons on the wings are MK32B-902E air refueling systems. The system consists of digital hose reel with a variable speed drogue enabling aerial refueling operations from one hundred to two hundred knots. The MC-130E/H models have been modified to accept this refueling system to provide a deep penetrating helicopter refueling role during special operations missions.

MC-130E/H Combat Talons are able to penetrate hostile airspace at low altitudes to carry out these missions. Talon crews are specially trained in night and adverse weather operations. It is well known that instrument flight rules, or IFR, govern ordinary aircraft flying through clouds. The Talons use their own version of IFR called *infrared* flight rules, which basically ignores all the rules and allows them to fly at high speeds at low levels in heavy ground fog or low cloud cover.

The MC-130H Combat Talon II features highly automated controls and displays that will reduce the crew size and workload. The flight deck as well as the cargo areas are compatible with night-vision goggles. The integrated control and display subsystem combines basic aircraft flight, tactical, and mission sensor data into a comprehensive set of display formats that assist each operator as he performs the tasks.

The pilot and co-pilot display formats include basic flight instrumentation and situational data. The display formats are available with symbology alone or with symbology overlaid with sensor video. The navigator uses radar ground map displays, FLIR display, tabular missions management display, and equipment status information. The EW officer's displays are used for viewing the EW data and to supplement the navigators in certain critical mission phases.

During Operation Desert Storm, the MC-130E Combat Talon I played a vital role. One-third of all air drops in the first three weeks of the war were carried out by MC-130s. The primary role was that of psychological operation, as it airdropped 11 BLU-82/B general-purpose bombs—a rather pedestrian name for a 15,000-pound bomb. Make no mistake, a 7 1/2-ton bomb makes quite an impression. When they exploded, a British SAS team radioed back to headquarters that "the Yanks are using nukes." Along with the bomb runs, the Talons also flew multiple mission air-dropping leaflets. A secondary role was in the CSAR missions.

MC-130E/H Specifications
Contractor: Lockheed; **powerplant:** four Allison turboprop engines T56-A15; **thrust:** 4,910 equivalent shaft power; **wingspan:** 132 feet, 7 inches (40.4 meters); **length:** MC-130E, 100 feet, 10 inches (30.7 meters); MC-130H, 99 feet, 9 inches (30.4 meters); **height:** 38 feet, 6 inches (11.7 meters);

speed: 300 miles per hour (at sea level); **range:** approximately 3,110 nautical miles, unlimited with air refueling; **ceiling:** 30,000 feet; **maximum takeoff weight:** 155,000 pounds (69,750 kilograms); **load:** MC-130E, 53 troops or 26 paratroops; MC-130H, 75 troops or 52 paratroops; **crew:** MC-130E, nine total—five officers (two pilots, two navigators, and one EW officer) and four enlisted (one flight engineer, two loadmasters, and one communications specialist); MC-130H, seven total—four officers (two pilots, one navigator, and one EW officer) and three enlisted (one flight engineer and two loadmasters).

MC-130W
The MC-130W is the newest addition to the AFSOC inventory. Its primary mission is the infiltration, exfiltration, and resupply of U.S. and allied Special Operations forces in direct support of unified and theater special operations commands and USSOCOM contingencies. Secondary missions include refueling of special operations rotary aircraft, forward arming and refueling (FARP), specialized ordnance delivery, airdrops in support of psychological operations, and limited command and control capabilities. Its global mission is primarily executed under the cover of darkness to reduce operational risk.

The aircraft is a modified C-130H(2) incorporating improved navigation, threat detection and countermeasures, and communication suites. The navigation suite is a fully integrated global positioning system (GPS)/inertial navigation system (INS) that interfaces with the AN/APN-241 low-power color radar and AN/AAQ-17 infrared detection system (IDS). The improved threat detection and countermeasures systems include advanced radar and missile warning receivers, chaff and flare dispensers and active infrared countermeasures, protecting the aircraft from both radar and infrared-guided threats. The communication systems upgrades include dual SATCOM suite with data burst capability. The aircraft has both interior and exterior night-vision goggle compatible lighting.

Structural improvements to the basic hercules aircraft include the addition of the universal aerial refueling receptacle slipway installation (UARRSI) and a strengthened tail empennage. The UARRSI allows the aircraft to conduct in-flight refueling as a receiver, and strengthening of the tail allows high speed low level aerial delivery system (HSLLADS) airdrop operations. The MC-130W is equipped with Mk32B-902E refueling pods. These pods are part of the most technologically advanced refueling system available and provide the ability to refuel special operations helicopters and the CV-22.

MC-130W Specifications

Primary mission: Infiltration, exfiltration, and resupply of Special Operations forces; also provides in-flight refueling of special operations vertical lift assets; **contractor:** Lockheed; **powerplant:** four Allison T56-A-15 turboprop engines; **thrust:** 4,910 shaft horsepower each engine; **Length:** 98 feet, 9 inches (30.09 meters); **height:** 38 feet, 6 inches (11.7 meters); **wingspan:** 132 feet, 7 inches (40.4 meters); **speed:** 300 miles per hour; **ceiling:** 33,000 feet (10,000 meters); **maximum takeoff weight:** 155,000 pounds (69,750 kilograms); **maximum normal payload:** 33,000 pounds; **maximum range with maximum normal payload:** 1,208 miles (1,050 NM), in-flight refueling extends this to unlimited range; **crew:** seven total—four officers, pilot, copilot, and two navigators and three enlisted (flight engineer, and two loadmasters).

MC-130P Combat Shadow

The Combat Shadow extends the range of special operations helicopters by providing air refueling. Operations are conducted primarily in formation, at night, at low level to reduce the probability of visual acquisition and interception by airborne threats. This is carried out in clandestine, low-level missions into politically sensitive or hostile territory. The Shadow is a visual flight rule (VFR) aircraft and would only be used when the pilots can see the ground, although penetrations are often aided by radar. The MC-130P may fly in a multi-ship or single-ship mission to reduce detection.

The secondary mission of the Combat Shadow includes the delivery of Special Operations forces. Small teams, assorted gear, equipment, Zodiacs, and combat rubber raiding craft (CRRC) are a few of the specialized items that are conveyed by the aircraft and its crew.

The Combat Shadow has a full IIN, GPS, and NVG-compatible lighting for the interior and exterior. This allows the crew to use NVG-compatible heads-up display (HUD)

A MC-130P, Combat Shadow. Note that this Shadow has had the STAR recovery arms removed from the nose. The MC-130P serves as an air refueling platform for SOCOM helicopters and can also be used as an insertion platform for STS teams as can be seen in the silhouettes of the team toward the rear of the aircraft.

to fly the plane. It has a FLIR, missile, and radar warning receiver to alert the crew of threats. Countermeasure devices include chaff and flare dispensers. Communications have satellite and data burst technology. In addition, the MC-130P will have in-flight refueling capability as a receiver.

Originally designated the HC-130 N/P, U.S. Air Force Special Operations aircraft were redesigned in February 1996 to correspond with all other M-series special operations aircraft.

MC-130Ps have been actively employed in special operations missions since the mid-1980s. These clandestine refuelers were deployed to Saudi Arabia to support Desert Storm in 1990. They provided the necessary air refueling of Special Operations forces helicopters. This was carried out in both coalition and hostile territory. Combat Shadows were also used in psychological operations and leaflet drops. One of these leaflets carried the following admonition to Iraqi troops:

Warning! This is only the beginning! This could have been a real bomb. We have no desire to harm innocent people, but Saddam is leading you to certain death and destruction. We want you to know the truth, Saddam is the cause. Yes, the Multi-National Forces have the ability to strike anywhere . . . and at anytime! Warning.

Such leaflets were responsible for hundreds of Iraqi troops surrendering without a shot being fired. During the

The refueling hose of this Combat Shadow is tucked into the pod. Upon its rendezvous with the hungry "choppers," it will extend the line and prepare to off load fuel as soon as the helicopters hook up their refueling probes.

The home office of the MC-130P. The flight deck. Here, the pilot, copilot, and flight engineer carry out the mission of getting their cargo delivered. In this case it is an STT and a RAMZ drop.

Although women are not allowed in STS teams, they may be found among the aircraft pilots and crewmembers, as in the case of this young major, a navigator on an MC-130P.

course of the war, the 8th Special Operations Squadron and the 9th SOS dropped more than seventeen million leaflets. Combat Shadows have also been employed as combat search and rescue as well as command and control aircraft.

MC-130P Specifications

Contractor: Lockheed; **powerplant:** four Allison turbo-prop engines T56-A 15; **thrust:** 4,910 equivalent shaft power; **wingspan:** 132 feet, 7 inches (40.4 meters); **length:** 97 feet, 9 inches (29.8 meters); **height:** 38 feet, 6 inches (11.7 meters); **speed:** 289 miles per hour (at sea level); **range:** approximately 4,000 nautical miles, unlimited with air refueling; **ceiling:** 33,000 feet; **maximum takeoff weight:** 155,000 pounds (69,750 kilograms, peacetime), 175,000 pounds (wartime); **crew:** eight total—four officers (pilot, copilot, primary navigator, and secondary navigator),

and four enlisted (flight engineer, communications operator, and two loadmasters).

EC-130E Rivet Rider Commando Solo

The Commando Solo, formally known as the Volant Solo, is flown by the 193rd Special Operations Group. It is the only AFSOC asset that is an Air National Guard entity. It has seen action from Operation Urgent Fury in 1983 during the assault on Grenada, to Operation Just Cause in 1989 in Panama. It served as the "Voice of the Gulf" during Operation Desert Storm in 1991, convincing Iraqi soldiers to surrender; and also in Operation Uphold Democracy in 1994 as a broadcasting platform during the Haitian uprising.

As the name implies, the Commando Solo works alone. It is capable of conducting day and night overt or covert operations. The primary mission of the EC-130 is to conduct

Senior Master Sgt. Tom Deffley directs the crew of an EC-130E Commando Solo aircraft of the 193rd SOW as they taxi out for takeoff on a mission over Iraq in 1998. The Commando Solo was deployed to the Southwest Asia area of operations in support of Operation Southern Watch, which is the U.S. and coalition enforcement of the no-fly-zone over Southern Iraq. During the GWOT, the aircraft would be deployed to broadcast messages to the local Afghan population and Taliban soldiers during Operation Enduring Freedom. Most recently, the Commando Solo has been deployed to the Middle East in support of Operation Iraqi Freedom. *U.S. Air Force*

The EC-130 Aircraft is jammed with electronic gear, from communications to telecommunications equipment. The country of Iraq is a prime area of operations for the Commando Solo. Since there is no FCC in the country, the crew has a free hand to exploit their skills to the fullest, whether it is operating a radio or television station. Here, members of the 4th Psychological Operations Group, 193rd Special Operations Wing, Pennsylvania Air National Guard, broadcast television and radio programming from onboard an ANG EC-130J "Commando Solo" aircraft, in support of Operation Iraqi Freedom. *U.S. Air Force*

psychological operations, civil affairs broadcast missions, and electronic countermeasures. This is accomplished by using standard AM/FM radio, HF/shortwave, TV, and tactical military communications frequencies while loitering outside the lethal range of any weapons possessed by enemy forces. The crew of the Commando Solo will carry out its PSYWAR mission both day and night, operating at the maximum altitudes to achieve maximum possible transmission into the given area of operation. Typical mission parameters will find a single EC-130E circling the target audience, whether it be military or civilian.

The EC-130 is not only capable of jamming enemy signals and communications, but it is also effective in pinpointing any attempts to jam communication by the enemy. Once the source is located, this information is passed on to the appropriate chain, and the electronic threat can be neutralized. If the enemy signal is something other than just noise, an alternate option would allow the enemy force to continue communicating and intercept their communications. Alternate missions include command and control, communications, countermeasures (C3CM), and occasionally intelligence gathering.

Overflowing with highly sophisticated electronics and mission-critical specialized modifications, the EC-130E incorporates enhanced navigation systems, self-protection equipment, secure fax machines, and computers. In addition to these devices, there are VCRs, cassettes, compact discs, and powerful transmitters that are capable of broadcasting color television on a multitude of worldwide standards, throughout the TV VHF/UHF ranges.

During the GWOT the EC-130 would again be pressed into service. The aircraft and crews perform a wide variety of missions. Whether the mission called for broadcasting messages to the Taliban and al-Qaeda forces in

Afghanistan, or dropping leaflets in Iraq, the Commando Solo would be on station.

In 2006 the E model was replaced by the J model, which featured enhanced navigation systems, self-protection equipment, air refueling, and the capability of broadcasting radio and color TV on all international standards.

EC-130E Specifications

Contractor: Lockheed; **powerplant:** four Allison turboprop engines T56-A15; **thrust:** 4,910 equivalent shaft power; **wingspan:** 132 feet, 7 inches (40.4 meters); **length:** 100 feet, 6 inches (30.9 meters); **height:** 38 feet, 6 inches (11.7 meters); **speed:** 299 miles per hour (at sea level); **range:** approximately 2,100 nautical miles (3,380 kilometers), unlimited with air refueling; **ceiling:** 20,000 feet; **maximum takeoff weight:** 155,000 pounds (69,750 kilograms); **crew:** 11 total—four officers (pilot, copilot, navigator, mission control chief/electronic warfare officer) and seven enlisted (flight engineer, loadmaster, and five mission crew).

EC-130J Specifications

Primary mission: Psychological and information operations; **Contractor:** Lockheed; **powerplant:** four Allison six-blade turboprop engines; **thrust:** 6,000 equivalent shaft power; **length:** 97.75 feet (29.7 meters); **height:** 38.8 feet (11.8 meters); **wingspan:** 132.6 feet (40.3 meters); **cruise speed:** 335 miles per hour; **ceiling:** 28,000 feet (8,534 meters); **maximum takeoff weight:** 155,000 pounds (69,750 kilograms); **range:** 2,300 nautical miles without refueling; **crew:** ten total—four officers, (pilot, copilot, flight systems officer, mission systems officer), and six enlisted (loadmaster, five electronic communications systems operators).

MH-53J Pave Low III E helicopter of the 20th SOS, call sign "Cowboy Zero-3." Having just dropped off a special tactics team and U.S. Army Rangers, the Pave Low prepares to take off and assume an orbit over the SOF operators. It will be on station to provide close air support (CAS) when called on by the team on the ground.

MH-53J Pave Low III

The mission of the MH-53J is to carry out low-level, long-range, undetected ingress into denied or hostile areas. This is accomplished day or night, even under the worst weather conditions for infiltration, exfiltration, and resupply of Special Operations forces.

Like its forerunner, the Sikorsky HH-53 Jolly Green Giant of the Vietnam era, the MH-53J Pave Low III Enhanced is the main helicopter in service with the Air Force Special Operations Command. Unlike its predecessor, it has been modified and augmented with state-of-the-art technology that the Jolly Green pilots would have killed for in their day.

The Pave Low is the largest and most powerful helicopter in the U.S. Air Force inventory and the most technologically advanced helicopter in the world. Forward-looking infrared, inertial GPS, Doppler navigation systems, a terrain-following/avoidance radar, an on-board computer, and integrated advanced avionics enable it to achieve precise, low-level, long-range penetration into denied areas, day or night, in adverse weather and over hazardous terrain without detection.

In the spring of 1999, AFSOC began modifying the MH-53J Pave Low with interactive defensive avionics system/multi-mission advanced tactical terminal (IDAS/MATT). This modification will provide the air crews with a heightened level of readiness and efficiency. The new designation for the Pave Low helicopters with this modification is the M model. This system is a color, multifunctional, night-vision-compatible, digital map screen. Located on the helicopter's instrument panel, the display gives the crew a more concise view of the battlefield and instant access to real-time events. The helicopter's flight path, manmade obstacles such as power lines, and even hostile threats "over the horizon" are depicted in an easy-to-read manner.

The system receives its data from a satellite, directly into the computer. The signal is then decoded and the data is displayed in 3D color imaging of the surrounding terrain, including contour lines and elevation bands. At the push of a button the crew can visualize a digital navigational course and bearing information, in addition to the map display. Designed to give crew members a priority in consolidating the variety of functions, extra detail was taken to provide the crew easy-to-control instrument panel functions while increasing the flow of information efficiently.

Newly upgraded MH-53M Pave Low, modified with the interactive defense avionics system/multi-mission advance tactical terminal (IDAS/MATT). Although regularly modified and upgraded, these helicopters are older than most of the crews flying them. For example, this helicopter was used on the Son Tay raid into North Vietnam.

All of this high technology results in what the U.S. Air Force calls the "crew concept"; the pilot of the MH-53J gets assistance from the copilot and flight engineer. These three individuals are crammed into the flight deck, smaller than an average-sized closet. Each one has his responsibility and a section of the controls to manage. Together, they make the Pave Low maneuver in such a way that staggers the imagination, and sometimes the stomach.

Offering protection to the crew is armor plating as well as an assortment of weapon systems. Just aft of the flight deck are two 7.62mm miniguns, and at the rear of the helicopter on the exit ramp is a .50-caliber machine gun. While the mission of the Pave Low is primarily an INFIL/EXFIL platform, with all the previously mentioned weapons, it also serves as a helicopter gunship. With a combination of armor, weaponry, and maneuverability, the crew is pretty well covered.

During Operation Desert Storm, an AFSOC MH-53J guided the U.S. Army AH-64 Apaches to their targets deep inside Iraq. Flying over hundreds of miles of featureless desert, the Air Commandos led the lethal sortie directly to two Iraqi early-warning radar stations. Here, the Apaches destroyed the Iraqi ground targets using Hellfire missiles. This opened a corridor for U.S. and coalition forces to begin the air war.

In addition to providing infiltration, exfiltration, and resupply of Special Operations forces, the Pave Lows provided CSAR coverage for Coalition Air Forces in Iraq, Saudi Arabia, Kuwait, Turkey, and the Persian Gulf. An MH-53J, call sign Moccasin 5, made the first successful combat recovery of a downed pilot in Desert Storm. At the conclusion of the war, the Pave Lows would see service in Northern Iraq to support Operation Provide Comfort, assisting the Kurds, and later on with IFOR operations in Bosnia.

The MH-53J Pave Low III heavy-lift helicopter is the largest, most powerful and technologically advanced helicopter in AFSOC's inventory. It is equipped with terrain-following and terrain-avoidance radar, forward looking infrared sensor, inertial navigation system with global positioning system, as well as a projected map display enabling the crew to follow terrain contours and avoid obstacles. These advanced avionics enable the aircraft to make low-level penetration into enemy territory possible. Mounted over the tanks is the direct infrared counter measure (DIRCM) anti-missile system. *U.S. Air Force.*

In the spring of 1999, AFSOC began upgrading the Pave Low with IDAS/MATT. IDAS improves combat survivability, provides flexible integrated EW, and incorporates existing defensive systems and a cockpit-mounted digital map system (DMS). MATT is a multi-service program, real-time over-the-horizon threat and intelligence data, real-time electronic order of battle alerts and updates, and integrates visual threat data onto cockpit avionics displays. The heart of IDAS/MATT is the DMS. This adds a cockpit-mounted color multi-function display; NVG compatible, multi-function display capability for existing pilot video monitors; to guide crews through mountainous terrain; digital map screen in various scales; visual flight plot management with waypoint look ahead capability; and visual display of threat and intelligence data. Those Pave Low helicopters having been modified are now designated "M" models.

As America presses the fight in the Global War on Terrorism, the Pave Low helicopters are instrumental in providing infiltration and exfiltration of U.S. Special Operations forces. Flying numerous sorties, the MH-53 helicopters have flown in SEALs and their fast attack vehicle, Special Forces ODA along with NSTV and special tactics teams with their all-terrain vehicles.

MH-53J Specifications

Contractor: Sikorsky Aircraft Corporation; **powerplant:** two General Electric T64-GE/100 engines; **thrust:** 4,339 shaft power per engine; **length:** 92 feet (27.88 meters); **height:** 25 feet (7.58 meters); **rotary diameter:** 72 feet (21.88 meters); **blades per hub:** six; **speed:** 195 miles per hour (312 kilometers per hour); **range:** 630 statute miles (548 nautical

Starboard gunner of the Pave Low engages the mini-gun. This 7.62mm minigun is capable of putting thousands of rounds per minute on target.

You will find no greater ride to get your heart pounding in AFSOC than on a Pave Low. The pilots of the 20th SOS can thread a needle with this ninety-two–foot helicopter. One Green Hornet pilot confesses that flying at treetop level, in the black of night, with NODs, although dangerous, is "kind of a cool thing!"

miles), unlimited with air refueling; **ceiling:** 16,000 feet (4,849 meters); **maximum takeoff weight:** 42,000 pounds (18,900 kilograms); **armament:** any combination of three 7.62mm miniguns and .50-caliber machine guns; **payload:** 38 fully equipped combat troops or 14 litters; its external cargo hook is also capable of 20,000 pounds (9,000 kilograms); **crew:** six total—two officers (pilots) and four enlisted (two flight engineers and two aerial gunners).

CV-22 "Osprey"

The Osprey is a tilt-rotor vertical lift aircraft, which means it takes off like a helicopter and flies like a conventional airplane. There is nothing conventional about the Osprey, however. Development of the V-22 program began in 1981 and was originally designed for the U.S. Marines, designated the MV-22. Planned for introduction into AFSOC forces in 2003, it was not until 20 March 2006, when the U.S. Air Force took delivery of the first operational CV-22, which is the special operations variant of the MV-22.

The Commander of Air Force Special Operations Command, Lt. Gen. Michael Wooly, commented, "I think its [CV-22] is going to truly transform the way we do business by giving us rapid mobility on the battlefield for our special operators that we have not had before."

The CV-22 differs from the MV-22 with the addition of a third seat in the cockpit for a flight engineer and can be fitted with a refueling probe to facilitate midair refueling. Additionally, the AFSOC version of the Osprey will have the modern suite of electronics, like those installed in other AFSOC aircraft, items such as a terrain-avoidance (TA) and terrain-following (TF) radar. To deal with the nature of special operations, it will have enhanced EW equipment for increased battlefield awareness, with more than 2.5 times the volume of flares and chaff, radar-jamming gear, and improved integration of defensive countermeasures. For CSAR it will have an internally mounted rescue hoist and a crew door located on the starboard side of the aircraft. Another significant difference between the AFSOC and marine version will be the amount of fuel it will carry. The CV-22 carries approximately twice the amount of fuel of the MV-22 variant.

Sources within AFSOC readily admit the Osprey was designed as a U.S. Marine aircraft, to fit inside a hanger deck of U.S. Navy LHD. One officer commented, "If we [the U.S. Air Force] had designed this aircraft it would have been larger, wider, and taller. If would be the same concept but more tactically feasible for the airlift/SOF mission."

The Osprey brings speed and range into the SOF arena. It is quick like the MC-130 and can hover like a MH-53. It allows the mission to be carried out in one period of darkness. Another benefit of the CV-22 is that it is quiet. One AFSOC officer relates, "It is like an A-10. You know it is up there, then wham! It is right on top of you. It is not like a regular helicopter where you hear the *whomp-whomp* sound of the rotor blades."

Currently, the Osprey is not armed, relying on its speed and stealth as its defense. However, there are evaluations underway to determine the possibility of adding a weapons system. The question remains, where would you place the weapon? If you position it on the starboard side, you would hit the large propellers. Mounting it on the rear ramp, you have a good chance of hitting the tail. There is discussion of a nose-mounted weapons system, but then that could affect the aerodynamics of the aircraft.

The $89 million (2005 dollars) CV-22 was to eventually replace AFSOC's entire fleet of MH-53 Pave Low and MH-60G Pave Hawk helicopters. Dispelling any rumors, the CV-22 was a replacement for the Pave Low; Brig. Gen. Michael Callan, commander of Air Force Special Operations forces (AFSOF), a warfighting command under AFSOC, stated, "It is not." There are even suggestions that it will phase out some of the MC-130E Combat Talon I and MC-130P/N Combat Shadows. However, with the introduction of the 160 SOAR(A) MH-47G and CV-22 models, the current direction of the Osprey will not be replacing the MC-130 class of aircraft anytime in the near future. Once deployed it is

The Osprey is a tilt-rotor aircraft that takes off and hovers like a helicopter then transitions to fly like an airplane. It is quick like an MC-130 and hovers like a Pave Low. Borne out of the ashes of Desert One, some call the Osprey the savior of special ops air platforms; time will tell whether the CV-22 is up to the challenging operational tempo of the SOF environment. One of the main advantages the CV-22 brings to the special operations arena is the ability to perform mission profiles in one period of darkness. *U.S. Air Force*

Operating with the 8th SOS, this unique aircraft is a dual-piloted, self-deployable, medium-lift, aircraft for joint service application. Its multi-engine tilt-rotor design combines the vertical flight capabilities of a helicopter with the speed and range of a fixed-wing airplane. Its primary mission is mobility, infiltration, exfiltration, and resupply of SOF operators around the globe. The aircraft is fully capable of operations in adverse weather, day or night, in climates from arctic to tropical, and in a variety of conventional, unconventional, and contingency combat situations, including nuclear, biological, and chemical (NBC) warfare conditions. *U.S. Air Force*

Capable of flying twenty-one hundred nautical miles with one aerial refueling, the CV-22 provides the services and advantages of V/STOL aircraft that can rapidly self-deploy to any location in the world. This would be beneficial for long-range SOF missions. In comparison, during Operation Enduring Freedom, special tactics teams and other SOF personnel were infiltrated via helicopters. This nine hundred–mile insertion required several mid-air refuelings of the helicopters; the CV-22 could have performed this mission with only one. *U.S. Air Force*

This view of the CV-22 shows how small the interior of the aircraft really is. The space is approximately equal to that of a CH-46 Sea Knight helicopter. The updated troop seats are made to withstand a crash landing. The Osprey can operate in a diverse environment; it will operate from aircraft-capable ships as well as shore sites ranging from main bases to austere forward operating locations. While an armed Osprey is being evaluated, the aircraft currently relies on speed and surprise to conduct its mission. *U.S. Air Force*

expected that fifty CV-22 Ospreys will replace up to eighty-nine current AFSOC aircraft. The mission of the CV-22 is to infil/exfil and resupply Special Operations forces in denied or enemy area in total darkness in all weather.

CV-22 Specifications

Primary missions: Special Operations forces mobility, long-range infiltration, exfiltration, and resupply under low-altitude, adverse weather, medium up to high threat environments; **contractor:** Bell Helicopter Textron, Inc., and Boeing Company, Defense and Space Group, Helicopter Division; **powerplant:** two Rolls Royce–Allison AE1107C turboshaft engines; **thrust:** 6,200 shaft horsepower per engine; **length:** 57 feet, 4 inches (17.4 meters); **height:** 22 feet, 1 inch (6.73 meters); **wingspan:** 84 feet, 7 inches (25.8 meters); **rotary diameter:** 38 feet (11.6 meters); **blades per hub:** three;

speed: 218 miles per hour (230 knots) (cruising speed); **ceiling:** 25,000 feet (7,620 meters); **maximum vertical takeoff weight:** 52,870 pounds (23,982 kilograms); **maximum rolling takeoff weight:** 60,500 pounds (27,443 kilograms); **self-deploy range:** 1,500 nautical miles with internal auxiliary fuel tanks and no refueling. More than 2,500 nautical miles is possible with one aerial refueling and auxiliary tanks; **payload:** 24 cargo troops, 12 litters or 20,000 pounds internal, external load of 10,000 pounds (4,536 kilograms) on single cargo hook, 15,000 pounds (9,221 kilograms) dual cargo hook; **crew:** four total—twp officers, pilot, copilot, and two enlisted (flight engineers).

U-28A

One of the newest additions being seen on the tarmac at Hurlburt Field is the U-28A. This single-engine aircraft is the

The CV-22 has a crew of four, with two pilots who sit side by side in the cockpit. It has the capability of providing a long-range infiltration/exfiltration platform for the special tactics teams as they head into the Global War on Terrorism. Early plans called for the aircraft to service as a replacement for AFSOC's fleet of MH-53 Pave Lows and some of the MC-130 aircraft. However, with the introduction of the MH-47G and CV-22 models, the current direction of the Osprey will not be replacing the MC-130 class of aircraft anytime in the near future. *U.S. Air Force*

military version of the Swiss-made Pilatus PC-12 transport. Its mission is to provide insertion and extraction support for Special Operations forces. The aircraft has a crew of two, but can be flown by one pilot.

The plane was selected for its versatile performance and ability to operate from short and unimproved runway surfaces. It is deployed when the airfields will not accommodate the larger MC-130 aircraft or due to the clandestine nature of the mission the smaller aircraft is more desirable.

Activated on 1 October 2005, the 319th Special Operations Squadron currently operates six U-28As, with approximately forty-five airmen to fly and maintain the aircraft. The turboprop U-28A can operate from shorter runways than a C-130, and, just like the larger aircraft, can land on austere fields such as dirt and grass strips. It can carry a payload of up to nearly three thousand pounds. The aircraft is equipped with weather radar and a suite of advanced communications and navigation gear.

U-28A Specifications

Primary mission: intra-theater support for Special Operations forces; **contractor:** Pilatus Air Ltd.; **powerplant:** one Pratt & Whitney PT6A-67B turboprop; **thrust:** 1,605 shaft horsepower (shp) flat-rated to 1,200 shp; **length:** 47 feet, 3 inches; **height:** 14 feet; **wingspan:** 53 feet, 3 inches; Max **cruise speed:** 270 knots true airspeed; **max payload:** 2,973 pounds; ceiling: 30,000 feet; **maximum takeoff weight:** 9,920 pounds; **ground roll:** 1,475 feet at max takeoff weight; **range:** 1,513 nautical miles; **crew:** two pilots; however, the aircraft can be flown by one.

MQ-1 Predator

The Air Force Special Operations Command reactivated the 3rd SOS on 28 October 2005; the squadron is known as the Dragons after the old Vietnam era AC-47 "Puff the Magic Dragon." AFSOC was tasked with the mission to fill the requirements for Predator full-motion video (FMV) to support the troops on the ground. By deploying the Predator, it brings all elements into play as SOF teams hunt down a wary and elusive enemy. The UAV allows for the acquisition of real-time target data transmitting back and forth between the UAV, command and control, the STS team on the ground and to orbiting AC-130 gunship or other CAS platforms.

In response, significant expansion to Predator operations is planned in the coming years and some of that support will be dedicated to SOF operations. AFSOC, as the air component of USSOCOM, maintains a close relationship with the command's SOF ground components. This personal level relationship is an important ingredient to effective operations. Fielding a Predator force structure within AFSOC represents the quickest, most cost-effective, most supportable, and most sustainable means of providing FMV support to SOF on the ground.

AFSOC currently operates the MQ-1; however, coming on line is the MQ-9 Reaper. The MQ-1 Predator is a "Killer Scout" where the MQ-9 Reaper is a "Hunter Killer." The Reaper is designed to hunt down high-value targets and destroy time-sensitive targets with persistence and precision. The MQ-9 is a completely different aircraft; three times as fast, it can fly twice as high, and can carry fifteen times the external payload. The primary mission of the Predator is armed reconnaissance. Though the full combat load of a MQ-9 will vary depending on the munitions selected, it can carry up to fourteen AGM-114 missiles as well as laser-guided bombs like the GBU-12.

The MQ-1 Predator is a medium-altitude, long-endurance, remotely piloted aircraft. The MQ-1's primary mission is interdiction and conducting armed reconnaissance against critical, perishable targets. The Predator brings persistent surveillance and strike without risking a manned

aircraft to the SOF area of operations. It is operated from a control van, officially called Mobile Ground Control Station; it is affectionately known as "dumpster." All members of the Predator control and support team are assigned to AFSOC. The personnel who operate the Predators are called pilots; and yes there are women on the Predator team. The basic crew is one pilot and two sensor operators.

Operational control of the UAV can be performed in theater or operated from within the continental U.S. During OEF, a special tactics team was in contact with the pilot of an MQ-1 providing them with imagery. The team leader inquired where the pilot was operating out of and he was told back in the states.

The entry of the UAV has brought one more level into the vertical battlespace (i.e., B-52s, AC-130, Helicopters, and CAS). The Predator team related: "Deconfliction with manned aircraft is a top priority. In theater, we communicate with the control and reporting center and are assigned altitudes just like any other aircraft. If necessary, we can move to allow strike aircraft to engage targets."

MQ-1 Predator Specifications

Primary missions: armed reconnaissance, airborne surveillance, and target acquisition; **contractor:** General Atomics Aeronautical Systems, Inc.; **powerplant:** Rotax 914 four cylinder engine producing 101 horsepower; **length:** 27 feet (8.22 meters); **height:** 6.9 feet (2.1 meters) **weight:** 1,130 pounds (512 kilograms) empty; **maximum takeoff weight:** 2,250 pounds (1,020 kilograms); **wingspan:** 48.7 feet (14.8

The MQ-9 Reaper is the U.S. Air Force's first hunter-killer UAV. It's larger and more powerful than the MQ-1 Predator and is designed to go after time-sensitive targets and destroy those targets with five hundred–pound bombs and Hellfire missiles. The Reaper can stay airborne for up to fourteen hours fully loaded and carries more than fifteen times the ordnance of the Predator, flying almost three times the Predator's cruise speed. *Courtesy of General Atomics Aeronautical Systems, Inc.*

meters); **speed:** Cruise speed around 84 mph (70 knots), up to 135 mph; **range:** up to 400 nautical miles (454 miles); **ceiling:** up to 25,000 feet (7,620 meters); **fuel capacity:** 665 pounds (100 gallons); **payload:** 450 pounds (204 kilograms); **armament:** AGM-114 Hellfire missiles.

MQ-9 Reaper Specifications

Primary missions: armed reconnaissance, airborne surveillance, and target acquisition; **contractor:** General Atomics Aeronautical Systems, Inc.; **powerplant:** Honeywell TPE-331-10T turboprop; 670 kW (900 shaft horse power); **length:** 36 feet (10.97 meters); **height:** 11 feet 8 inches (3.56 meters); **weight:** 10,000 pounds (4540 kilograms); **wingspan:** 66 feet (20.12 meters); **speed:** Cruise speed around 405 km/h mph (220 knots); **ceiling:** up to 25,000 feet (7,620 meters); **Armament:** AGM-114 Hellfire missiles and GBU-12 laser-guided bombs.

Chapter 6

SPECIAL TACTICS SQUADRONS

The U.S. Army has the Rangers and the Special Forces (the Green Berets). In the U.S. Navy the special operators are the SEALs and special boat teams. Rounding out the full force of the U.S. Special Operations forces on the ground are the men of the U.S. Air Force Special Operations Command special tactics squadrons. Referred to as special tactics teams (STTs), they are a combination of combat controllers, pararescuemen and, on occasion, Special Operations weather teams. The STT is an integral part of the U.S. Special Operations Command and its missions. STT members frequently operate with the U.S. Navy SEALs, U.S. Army Rangers, and U.S. Army Special Forces units in SR, CSAR, and DA (i.e., airfield seizure), to name just a few of their capabilities. Every member of the STS teams is a volunteer. These highly motivated, proficient STTs are capable of being deployed by sea, air, or land often weighed down with one hundred to one hundred fifty pounds of equipment to execute their mission. These units will be found regularly on missions alongside the U.S. Army and U.S. Navy SOF troops. Whether they fast rope in with a company of Rangers, perform a high-altitude low-opening (HALO) parachute in with a Special Forces "A-team," or insert via submarine with a SEAL platoon, STS teams are qualified in these skills and add a lethal element to U.S. Special Operations forces.

Special Tactics Combat Control and Pararescue

Operating under the AFSOC, the special tactics squadrons are comprised of combat controllers and pararescuemen. These men are proficient in sea-air-land insertion tactics into forward, nonpermissive environments. The CCTs establish assault zones with an air traffic control capability. Assault zones could be a drop zone for a parachute deployment, a landing zone for heliborne operations, or a follow on fixed-wing aircraft. It could also be an extraction or low-level resupply.

The CCTs specialize in air traffic control. When it is given the "go" signal, it can place numerous forms of lights—visible and infrared—that can be controlled by CCT members as easily as you would use your TV remote on your home theater system. The combat control teams are also responsible for ground-based fire control of the AC-130 gunships and helicopters of AFSOC, as well as for all air assets, including U.S. Army and Navy aircraft. In addition to these capabilities, CCTs provide vital command and control capabilities in the forward AO and area qualified in demolition to remove obstructions and obstacles to the landing or drop zone.

The ratio of CCTs to PJs will vary with the mission profile and who the STT will be attached with (i.e., Rangers, SEALs, Special Forces, and so on). If the mission is a combat search and rescue, then the team would be pararescue jumper "heavy"; whereas, if the task is to take down an airfield and hold it, the team would then be made up primarily of CCTs. Each mission profile is unique and the special tactics teams are highly skilled in overcoming, adapting, and improvising to meet their objectives.

While the combat controllers are busy with their tasks, the PJs provide any emergency medical care necessary to stabilize and evacuate injured personnel. The PJs are the ones who will establish the overall combat search and rescue operations, planning, and procedures. The pararescuemen of the STS will provide triage and medical treatment for follow-on forces. To say that these individuals are highly skilled would be an understatement. They are instructed in the latest

Left: Skilled in the art of small unit tactics, a CCT and PJ patrol though the brush performing a reconnaissance and surveillance, or R and S. With the weapons at the ready, they are poised to engage any threat crossing their path.

medical procedures in combat and trauma medicine. When they are not jumping into remote hostile environments, or in training in a joint task force field training exercise (FTX), you might find them riding along with EMS units in large urban areas. Such cities have high incidents of gunshot wounds and similar injuries, so they may get further experience to take into the field.

During Operation Just Cause, the special tactics squadrons were with the Rangers in the raid on Rio Hato. CCTs perform air traffic control and special air assets fire control. PJs were there to provide emergency medical assistance and triage evaluation with the Rangers. CCT members were also with SEAL Team 4 at Patilla Airport.

Special tactics squadrons are a combination of combat controllers, pararescuemen, and at times Special Operations weathermen. These highly trained battlefield airmen are experts in ATC, CAS, and emergency trauma medicine. They can often be found attached with U.S. Army Special Forces, Rangers, and U.S. Navy SEALs, and have been known to operate with SAS units. *U.S. Air Force*

CCTs provided the air traffic control in Saudi Arabia and virtually ran the King Fihad Airport during Desert Shield. At the beginning of "The Storm" they conducted missions that assisted in opening the air corridor for U.S. and coalitions aircraft.

Members of the 24th STS were with Task Force Ranger in Somalia. For their actions during the firefight, combat controller Tech. Sgt. Tim Wilkinson was awarded the U.S. Air Force Cross for extraordinary heroism, Master Sgt. Jeffery Bray, and Master Sgt. Scott C. Fales, both PJs, received Silver Stars for gallantry.

During Operation Restore Democracy, while network news crews showed the U.S. helicopters settling into an LZ in Haiti and being heralded as "the first Americans to land on Haitian soil," members of the AFSOC/STS had already been on the ground for days, surveying HLZ and setting up lighting for the heliborne troopers.

There are six STS units worldwide, with approximately three hundred combat controllers and pararescue jumpers combined throughout the U.S. Air Force. The 21st STS is stationed at Fort Bragg, North Carolina; the 24th STS is at Pope Air Force Base, North Carolina; the 22nd STS is at McChord Air Force Base, Washington; the 23rd is at Hurlburt Field, Florida; the 320th STS is at Kadena Air Base, Japan; and the 321st STS is at RAF Mildenhall, England. Each squadron has three teams; each team comprises 18 enlisted and two officers. One half of the team will be qualified as combat controllers and the other half pararescue. Currently, there are more combat controllers in the squadron than there are PJs.

Pararescue Origins

Today's pararescuemen can trace their lineage back to a remote jungle close to the China-Burma border during a summer in World War II. Here, 21 persons were forced to bail out of a disabled C-46 in the hot month of August 1943. The area was so isolated that the only possible way to get to the survivors was a parachute drop. Lt. Col. Don Fleckinger, along with two medical personnel, volunteered to make the jump. From this mission the concept of pararescue was born.

In the early fifties, with the formation of the Air Rescue Service, and subsequently in 1956, into the reorganized Air

Rescue and Recovery Service, PJs, or *para-jumpers* as the name denotes, have been prepared to make the ultimate sacrifice to uphold their motto, "That others may live." Trained in parachuting, mountaineering, and medical techniques, these men would provide the rescue capability for both military and civilian rescues.

U.S. Air Force PJs have also been instrumental in the recovery of astronauts in the space program of the United States. Pararescuemen have worked with NASA since the early Gemini programs of the sixties. They were present to support Skylab missions and currently are on call to provide rescue support to the space shuttle program.

It was in 1966 that U.S. Air Force Chief of Staff Gen. John P. McConnell approved the wearing of the maroon beret for pararescue forces. The maroon beret symbolizes the blood sacrifices by PJs and their devotion to duty in coming to the aid of others.

A considerable benefit to the PJs was the introduction of combining parachuting capability with scuba techniques. It is not uncommon for a pararescueman to be loaded with up to one hundred pounds of equipment when he is ready to make his jump. According to Master Sgt. Ron Childress (ret.), "It was not uncommon for the PJs to put the survivor on the penetrator under heavy fire and be killed in action . . . to effect the survivor recovery."

During the Vietnam War, PJs accompanied the Jolly Green helicopters in the search and rescue of downed pilots. These men operated the jungle penetrators as well as the onboard weapons. It was not uncommon for a PJ to ride the hoist down to an injured pilot, with M-16 in hand, and secure the wounded man to the penetrator and hold him secure as they rode back up to the relative safety of the hovering helicopter.

During Operation Just Cause in 1989, pararescuemen were among the first U.S. combatants to parachute into Panama. Their medical expertise was called upon continually during this short operation, as they recovered and treated the majority of U.S. Army Rangers who had taken two Panamanian airfields in the first hours of the invasion. Speeding up and down the runway in their specially designed rescue all-terrain transport (RATT), the PJs collected the casualties and brought them to a collection point. At this location the pararescuemen performed triage and provided the necessary medical attention until MedEvac could be arranged. All this time firefights were going on around them while they cared for their wounded.

The PJs were on call during Operations Desert Shield and Desert Storm in the Persian Gulf. It was during the Gulf War that the pararescuemen would penetrate into hostile territory to recover a downed F-14 navigator. Pararescue also provided support for the airlift operations after the war to the Kurdish refugees fleeing into northern Iraq.

In the Global War on Terrorism, the PJs continued to carry out their mission in Operations Enduring Freedom and Iraqi Freedom. The training of a pararescueman is a constant process. They continuously endeavor to perfect current techniques as well as develop new procedures. Whether scaling the face of a mountain, doing a HALO jump at twenty-five

Having reached their recon position, this combat controller uses a PRC-117 SATCOM radio to communicate information back to headquarters. Across his knee rests his M4A1 rifle, just in case.

thousand feet, racing down the tarmac of some foreign airfield, or suspended from a cable of an MH-53 Pave Low over a distressed vessel in the Pacific, the PJs will accomplish their tasks at all costs.

CCT Origins

The need for combat controllers surfaced in the early air campaigns of World War II. During several major parachute assaults, the paratroopers fell short of their drop zone. This resulted in troopers being scattered as much as thirty miles from the drop zone. It became quite evident that effective guidance and control of the air transports were required. The U.S. Army created and trained a company-sized group of scouts who were parachute qualified. This unit became known as Pathfinders. Their mission was to precede the main assault force to the drop zone. Once on the ground they would use lights, flares, and smoke pots to provide a visual guide and weather information to the incoming planes.

In the fall of 1943 Pathfinders were first employed during the airborne reinforcement of allied troops in Italy. Minutes before the main body reached the designated area, the Pathfinders hit the ground and established the drop zone for the follow-on paratroops. These CCT forerunners, the Pathfinders, proved instrumental in the D-day invasion of Europe as they prepared the way for elements of the 82nd and 101st Airborne Divisions.

On 18 September 1947 the U.S. Air Force was officially established. The air force assumed responsibility for tactical airlift support of U.S. Army forces. Air force Pathfinders were later called combat control teams and were activated in January 1953. This newly organized group provided navigational aids and air traffic control for the expanding airlift forces. These teams remained under aerial port squadrons until 1977. In 1984, CCTs were restructured and assigned to the numbered U.S. Air Forces (e.g., 8th Air Force), and in 1991 they were placed under the control of host wing commanders.

Since their activation, CCTs have seen action worldwide. Combat controllers participated in the Lebanon crisis (July–October 1958), the Congo uprising (July–October 1960), the Cuban Missile Crisis (October 1962), the China-India confrontation (November 1962–September 1963), and during the Vietnam War (1967–1975).

It was also during the Vietnam War that the CCTs emerged as one of the U.S. Air Force's premiere units. Their exploits in Southeast Asia helped form the basis of current combat control operating methods. They were qualified as air traffic controllers, parachutists, and in emergency first aid. They also received training in communications, small unit patrolling techniques, and ambush and counter-ambush tactics. It was the CCTs who established drop zones and landing zones. Here, the basis of operating methods was developed and refined as used by today's combat control teams.

Combat control teams could be found collocated in isolated U.S. Army Special Forces camps scattered throughout Vietnam. Here, these air commandos called in air strikes to support the Green Beret camps, or guide a C-123 Fairchild or C-130 Hercules down the airstrip for a much-needed resupply run. Such beginnings have evolved into the close bond between the STS units and other Special Operations forces.

It has been reported that combat control teams were used in clandestine missions near the Ho Chi Minh Trail. These special operations troops would locate enemy convoys, then call in Air Commando gunships, such as "Puff," "Spooky," or other Spectres, to attack the column, thus severing the Communist supply line to the south and the North Vietnamese Army (NVA).

From 1967 through 1972 combat controllers saw action throughout the Vietnam theater of operations. They ensured mission safety, expedited air traffic flow, and coordinated with airlift control units. CCTs were the last troops to be evacuated from the beleaguered outpost at Khe Sahn. Two U.S. Air Force combat controllers were among the last Americans to be airlifted from the U.S. Embassy when Saigon fell in 1975.

Prior to Operation Eagle Claw, a lone combat controller performed reconnaissance and surveillance (R&S) of Desert Site One. The mission planners had scores of aerial photographs, but they needed HUMINT, someone on the ground. In early April 1980, Maj. John T. Carney, Jr., was delivered to the Iranian wasteland via a Central Intelligence Agency aircraft.

The major pulled a small motorcycle from the plane. Equipped with a pair of night-vision goggles, a shovel, and some beacons, he began to survey the proposed landing site. Major Carney paused from time to time to take a core sample of the desert sand. This was later analyzed to determine if the location could support the weight of the Sea Stallions and Hercules that would bring in Colonel Beckwith's rescue force.

It was for this mission that the "box and one" lighting method was deployed. Setting up his strobes in a box pattern approximately ninety feet apart, then placing the fifth at the end of the landing zone five thousand feet away, he marked the end of the LZ. Thus, Major Carney's team of combat controllers had given him a tool where five strobes would do the job that was normally done by more than two dozen. With the light bags burred below the surface, Carney took one more survey of the area before loading his motorcycle into the CIA Otter and extracting from Iran.

When the aircraft containing the assault force arrived for the actual mission, the pilots hit the remote and the five lights lit up the landing zone below. The mission of the combat controller was a success, one of the few of Operation Eagle Claw. Operation Rice Bowl, the planning of the rescue mission and the successful execution of the R&S by Major Carney, is viewed by those in the AFSOC as the birth of the special tactics teams.

Combat controllers jumped with the U.S. Army Rangers in Grenada in Operation Urgent Fury in 1983 and again as the United States invaded Panama in 1989 in Operation Just Cause. While their PJ teammates tended the wounded, CCTs called in air strikes from AC-130H gunships in support of the Rangers' operations. Combat controllers would be with the Rangers and Delta in support of Task Force Ranger in Somalia.

After the 9/11 attacks, combat controllers were among the first U.S. Special Operations forces on the ground in Afghanistan. In support of Operation Enduring Freedom the controllers were often attached to U.S. Army Special Forces ODA to provide CAS against the Taliban and al-Qaeda forces. They are also active in various missions in Operation Iraqi Freedom.

Whether it was on a trodden-down cow pasture in Europe in World War II where they lit smoke pots to mark the landing field, an isolated Special Forces camp in the central highland of Vietnam, or prosecuting GOWT in the wasteland of Afghanistan, combat controllers have been and continue to be an integral part of the success of special operations.

Today, combat control teams are ground combat forces assigned to the special tactics squadrons of the U.S. Air Force Special Operations Command. These highly trained CCTs are organized and equipped to establish and control the air-ground interface in the objective area rapidly. These functions include assault zone assessment and establishment,

The extreme in low-level insertion, going in on foot. STT are trained to utilize GPS, maps, a compass, and even the stars to navigate from point-to-point to accomplish their mission. If you look under the floppy hats, you can see the "secrette," this is the communications headgear used with the inter-team radios. These two STS team members wear a new type of 3D camouflage. This "cammo" has leaf patterns attached to break up any silhouette and allow them to disappear into the surrounding foliage.

The water, like special operations, is unforgiving. Those going into STS will learn the latest techniques in open circuit SCUBA and close circuit, as the Draeger re-breather. Here a combat controller emerges from the water wearing a LAR-V re-breather. The LAR-V will leave no telltale bubbles on the water's surface to give away the STT location during an underwater insertion.

Special tactics teams receive Military Free Fall training at Ft. Bragg and Yuma Proving Grounds. Wearing a Gentex helmet with oxygen in place, this PJ is armed with a Colt M4A1 carbine and an ACOG scope mounted on top, in place of the carrying handle, which is part of the SOPMOD kit.

air traffic control command and control communications, and special operations terminal attack control. In the event that the runway or airfield must be cleared of obstacles, the CCT units are trained in removal and equipped with demolitions that allow them to accomplish such a task. Combat control teams may be deployed with air and ground forces in the execution of direct action, special reconnaissance, austere airfield, combat search and rescue, counterterrorism, foreign internal defense, and humanitarian assistance operations.

Combat controllers' roles and responsibilities are to plan, organize, supervise, and establish air traffic control at forward airheads. They will select or assist in selecting sites and marking assault zones (drop, landing, or recovery)

with visual and electronic navigational aids for day and night air-land and air-drop operations. The CCT will operate portable and mobile communications equipment and terminal and en route air navigation aids required to control and support air traffic in these forward areas. These teams will evaluate and relay the status of assault zones to inbound aircraft as well as higher headquarters. Such reports may include limited weather observations, including surface and altitude wind data, temperature, and cloud heights. CCTs control vehicular traffic in the airport area, in the air, and on the runway and taxiways. They also monitor air navigational aids and maintain qualification of primary assigned weapons.

Land navigation is essential to the skills of an STS member. Both PJs and combat controllers will become experts in using a map and a compass. They will also become familiar with celestial navigation. While they are issued GPS units and are quite adapt in their use, they must always be able to travel from point-to-point relaying on low-tech alternatives.

The CCT on the ground is "the" air traffic controller. He regulates en route and airhead air traffic and initiates, coordinates, and issues air traffic control clearances, holding instructions, and advisories to maintain aircraft separation and promote safe, orderly, and expeditious air traffic flow under visual or non-radar flight rules. Whether using the radio in his truck or the tactical air navigation (TACAN) unit attached to the rear of a quad, he conducts ground-to-air communication. Visual and electronic systems are used to control and expedite the movement of aircraft while en route, arriving, and departing from the airhead. The CCT will interface with pilots, issuing advisories on air traffic control, weather, and wake turbulence. He directs actions in handling aircraft emergencies during special tactics team deployments to support contingency operations. He'll coordinate clearances, instructions, advisors, and air traffic movement with forward and rear area commanders. Combat controllers are instrumental in providing close air support with AFSOC assets. Combat controllers may receive advance training and become qualified in Special Operations tactical air control (SOTAC), allowing them to provide CAS with the "fast movers."

Further, the CCT establishes and operates forward communication facilities and supervises and establishes high-frequency, satellite, or other long-range C41 links between forward and rear area commanders. The CCT will develop terminal instrument procedures for assault zones, including gathering current ground intelligence in forward airhead areas. Combat controllers coordinate with pararescue personnel on casualty and patient staging and collection point for expeditious medevac.

Special tactics squadron combat controllers may be deployed into forward area and forward operating locations in special operation missions, personnel recovery, CSAR, and fire support duties. Along with the removal of obstacles with explosives, there may be an occasion when the CCT would be called upon to "sanitize" a crash site. While the task of "blowing up" a downed aircraft normally falls under the responsibility of other operators (e.g., Rangers, SEALs, Special Forces, and so on), CCTs are fully capable of carrying out such a task if necessary. The special tactics CCTs are definitely one of the USSOCOM's most lethal weapons.

10th Combat Weather Squadron

Assigned to the 720th Special Tactics Squadron is the 10th Combat Weather Squadron. Its mission is to provide meteorological and oceanographic information in and for the special operations theater of operations. Their functions include tactical infiltration, data collection, analysis and forecasting, mission tailoring of environmental data, and operating jointly with a host nation's weather personnel. CWS personnel perform this job from a forward-deployed base or at times from behind enemy lines using tactical weather equipment and an assortment of communications equipment.

CWS operates with subordinate units of the U.S. Army's Special Operations Command (USASOC), Special Forces Command (USASFC), and Civil Affairs/Psychological Operations Command (USACAPOC). The CWS trains and maintains readiness of assigned forces to conduct special combat operations anytime, anywhere, independently, or attached to USASOC units.

The combat weather squadron can trace its lineage to air and ground combat and Special Operations since 1943. One of the earliest commanders of the squadron was Lt. Col. (later Brig. Gen.) Richard Ellsworth. He and the 10th WS operated with Col. Phillip Cochran's 1st Air Commando Group, Brig. Orde Wingates Chindit's (long-range penetration teams), and Brig. Gen. Frank Merrill's 5037th Composite Infantry Provisional ("Merrill's Marauder"). The nature of weather on operations in the China-Burma-India Theater demanded the use of small weather teams inserted to provide observations from deep within enemy territory.

In June 1966 the 10th WS was reactivated at Udorn Airfield, Thailand, to conduct combat weather operations in Southeast Asia. The squadron also trained indigenous personnel and set up clandestine weather observation networks throughout the region. Tenth Weather Squadron personnel were key players in many successful special operations, including the Son Tay raid, America's attempt to rescue POWs from a prison camp in North Vietnam. Timing for the "raid" was advanced by twenty-four hours based on the forecast done by 10th WS.

Special Operations weather teams provide time-sensitive forecasting with a direct effect on a combatant commander's decisions. During one of the first airdrops into Afghanistan, with less than an hour before the drop a dust storm threatened to abort the insertion. The SWOT on the ground radioed back, "Sit tight. This will pass in about fifteen minutes." The MC-130 aircraft loaded with 75th Regiment Rangers continued on its flight plan. Just as the weathermen had forecasted, the dust storm cleared up and the Rangers were able to carry out their jump. *U.S. Air Force*

On 1 April 1996, the 10th Weather Squadron was redesignated the 10th Combat Weather Squadron (10th CWS) at Fort Bragg, North Carolina. This one squadron is comprised of five detachments located within the United States and two separate overseas operating locations. Special Operations forces supported by the 10th CWS include U.S. Army Special Forces, U.S. Army Rangers, 160th Special Operations Aviation Regiment, special warfare training groups, and special operations support battalions. Assigned to AFSOC, the Special Operations weather technicians go through a limited version of the pipeline.

The Pipeline

Whether an airman comes into the pipeline from U.S. Air Force Basic Military Training or volunteers from current Air Force Specialty Codes (AFSC), he will go through a selection process. Upon successful completion, the candidate will then follow a specific pipeline based on his choice of specialty. In the past both potential combat controllers and pararescuemen shared the same pipeline for core training, parting from the path to attend their specialty schools. Today, each of the battlefield airmen has a unique pipeline, though, at times, their paths may intertwine.

Battlefield airmen assigned to the 10th Combat Weather Squadron wear a grey beret. Shown here is their crest and beret flash. The three-colored stripes are representative of green for Army, purple for Joint Operations, and blue for Air Force.

Combat Controller Pipeline

Combat control orientation—two weeks; Air Traffic Control School, Keelser AFB, Mississippi—sixteen weeks; U.S. Army Airborne School, Fort Benning, Georgia—three weeks; Survival School and Dunker training, Fairchild AFB, Washington—three weeks; Combat Control School, Pope AFB, North Carolina—twelve weeks; Advanced Skills Training, Hurlburt Field, Florida—fifty-two weeks; Military Free Fall School, Fort Bragg, North Carolina, and Yuma, Arizona—four weeks; and U.S. Air Force Combat Dive School, Panama City, Florida—six weeks.

Pararescue Pipeline

Pararescue Indoctrination, Lackland AFB, Texas—twelve weeks; U.S. Air Force Combat Diver School, Panama City, Florida—six weeks; U.S. Army Airborne School, Fort Benning, Georgia—three weeks; Military Free Fall School, Fort Bragg, North Carolina, and Yuma, Arizona—four weeks; Survival School and Dunker training, Fairchild AFB, Washington—three weeks; Pararescue Medical Training, Kirtland AFB, New Mexico—twenty-two weeks; and Pararescue Rescue Training, Kirtland AFB, New Mexico—twenty weeks.

Special Operations Weatherman Pipeline

Weather School, Kessler AFB, Mississippi—twenty-six weeks. Upon successful completion the airman is assigned to a conventional weather unit. After two years he can volunteer for Special Operations Weatherman training. If selected he continues the pipeline: U.S. Army Airborne School, Fort Benning, Georgia—three weeks; Survival School and Dunker training, Fairchild AFB, Washington—three weeks; and Advanced Skills Training (Phases 3 and 4), Hurlburt Field, Florida.

The Pipeline Core Schools

U.S. Army Airborne School, Fort Benning, Georgia. Here for the next three weeks trainees will be at the mercy of the U.S. Army's "Black Hats," the Airborne instructors of the 1st Battalion (Airborne), 507th Parachute Infantry Regiment, who will convert a "leg" into an "Airborne" trooper. They will

learn what it takes to hurl oneself out of a perfectly good airplane for the purpose of infiltrating into a mission drop zone.

Basic airborne training is broken into three weeks: Ground, Tower, and Jump Week. During Ground Week our trainees will start an intensive program of instruction designed to prepare the troopers to complete their parachute jumps. They will learn how to execute a flawless parachute landing fall (PLF) to land safely in the LZ. The PLF consists of five points of contact designed to absorb the shock of landing and distribute it across the (1) balls of the feet, (2) calf, (3) thigh, (4) buttocks, and (5) the push-up muscle of the back. They will learn the proper way to exit an aircraft using mockups of a C-130 and C-141. They will climb up a thirty-four-foot tower; here, they will be connected to the lateral drift apparatus (LDA) and upon command will assume door position and "Jump!" Proper body position will be evaluated, and they'll do it over and over until the "Black Hats" are happy; and they will run.

Next comes Tower Week. Now that our trainees have learned how to exit, position, and land, they will have this week to refine those skills. Using a training device known as the swing landing tower (SLT) where they are hooked up to a

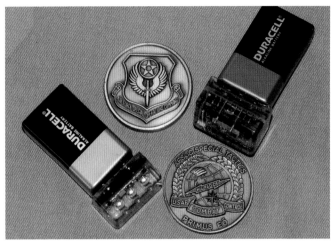

Above: The Phoenix IR transmitter, weighing a mere two ounces, is a pocket-size user-programmable infrared (IR) beacon designed for personal combat identification (CID). Invisible to the naked eye, when observed with NVG it can be seen up to five miles away. A nine-volt battery, lightweight and easy to use, powers the transmitter. The Phoenix Jr. is a simple on/off strobe. The other unit contains two protruding pins allowing the unit to be programmed with a varying series of patterns.

Left: Seen here are two MS-2000(M) Strobe lights, which has replaced the SDU-5/E. This omni-directional white light is equivalent to 250,000 lumens. The light on the right has the IR (infrared) shield in place, which is visible only with NVGs. The unit on the left has the cover off. The strobe also features a blue filter, which differentiates the signal of the strobe from ground fire. The strobe is useful to facilitate CAS, PR, and other ground-to-air signaling. While common among all SOF units, CCT will carry a number of them to facilitate ground-to-air signaling.

Below: While STS teams are equipped with the latest high-tech equipment, the venerable smoke grenade also has its place in the rucksacks and assault vest of these elite troopers. It is not unusual to find a smoke grenade or two attached to an Air Commando's LBE or assault vest for signaling positions, or marking an HLZ for pickup. Seen here is an assortment of M18 colored smoke grenades in violet, yellow, and green (not shown but also available is red). The grenade produces a cloud of colored smoke for fifty to ninety seconds.

parachute harness, they jump from a twelve-foot-high elevated platform. The apparatus provides the downward motion and oscillation simulating that of an actual parachute jump. To make things more challenging for the student, the instructors have control of the SLT and can determine if they want to land hard or soft. As one student rushes toward the ground, hands clinging to the harness, the instructor yells, "Hazard left!" and leans into the rope controlling the drop. They watch as the airborne trainee hits the ground, and they better have landed in a manner to avoid the imaginary obstacle, or the "Airborne Sergeant" will have a few choice words and a number of push-ups, too. "Airborne!"

During week two the student gets to ride the "Tower." The Tower is designed to give the student practice in controlling the parachute during the decent from 250 feet and execute a PLF upon landing. They will learn how to handle parachute malfunctions, and they will run.

Armed with the GUU-5/P and M203 grenade launcher, this STT team leader provides cover as his team settles in for a regional survey. Note he is wearing three strobes: one pouch attached to his ALCIE pack strap, one secured to his LBE, and a third sewn to the sleeve of his BDU. No matter how much equipment he may have to dump, he will still be able to execute his mission, and if necessary, evade and escape (E&E) out of enemy territory.

Combat Controller Staff Sgt. Rick Driggers listens to the pilot of "Cowboy Zero-3," an incoming Pave Low that will provide CAS to his STS team. Driggers wears an integrated ballistic helmet. This helmet is being evaluated as a replacement for the Gentex helmets now in use. The IBH is a Kevlar helmet with communications gear attached to the headgear.

Finally, week three, Jump Week. The potential STS trooper will perform five parachute jumps. First, an individual jump with a T-10B. Next, a mass exit with equipment and T-10B chute. Then another individual exit with MC1-1B parachute and tactical assembly. The fourth jump will be a mass exit at night with T-10B and tactical equipment, and finally the fifth jump either an individual jump with an MV1-1B or mass jump with a T-10B parachute.

The U.S. Army's "Guide for Airborne Students" states, "Airborne training is a rite of passage for the warrior." Upon graduation they will be awarded the coveted silver wings and are now qualified as "Airborne" troopers.

U.S. Army Military Freefall Parachutist School. The mission of the school is to train personnel in the science of HALO, military free-fall parachuting, and using the Ram-Air Parachute System (RAPS). Military free-fall (MFF) parachuting enables the theater commander to infiltrate an STS team into an area that would prohibit the use of static-line parachute operations. Special operations missions require rapid and covert infiltration into operational areas.

During week one, the future STS members will go through the normal in-processing and be issued equipment. At this time they will be assigned to a HALO instructor who will remain with them throughout the four-week training

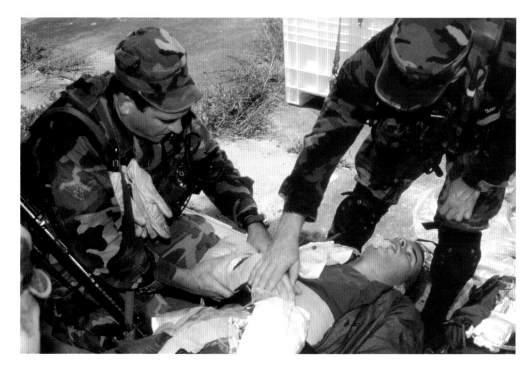

"PJ Forward!" Working together, a Ranger pitches in to assist the STS Pararescuemen as they tend to an injured crew member. The PJs of AFSOC are among the highest trained medical specialist in SOCOM. While their mission is to aid the injured, they are combatants and keep their weapons, a CAR-15 and MP5, close at hand.

cycle. It is also during week one that they will be matched up with a "jump buddy." Their buddy will be approximately the same weight and height so they will fall at the same rate.

In ground school they will learn about the ram-air parachutes, substantially different from the usual T-10B or MC1-1B that they jumped with at Basic Airborne School. The MC-5 ram-air parachutes are rectangular as opposed to circular. These parachutes are much more maneuverable. Repacking procedures as well as rigging the parachutes and equipment will be taught in this phase of training. At this time, special jump commands will be covered as well as the use of the oxygen systems used for high-altitude jumping.

Emergency procedures (EPs) such as parachute malfunctions, cut-aways, entanglements, and so on are taught, and so is how to recover from these mishaps. These exercises are run through over and over until they become second nature to the jumpers. Falling at a rate of more than one hundred eighty feet per second, you do not have the luxury of thinking about the problem, you must react.

While in week one, the candidate will spend time in the Military Free Fall Simulator Facility. Completed in 1992 at Fort Bragg, at a cost of $5 million, this eleven thousand-square-foot facility contains an enclosed, vertical wind tunnel, thirty-two-student classroom, operator control room, communications, and equipment rooms. "This facility is a marked

improvement," relates Carol Darby of the Special Warfare School. "Prior to having the facility, the students had to practice [body stabilization] by lying on tabletops."

The simulator is approximately eighteen feet high and fourteen feet in diameter and can support two jumpers with equipment up to three hundred seventy five pounds. The simulator's fan generates winds up to one hundred thirty two miles per hour. Suspended in a column of air, the students will learn and practice body-stabilization techniques. The wind tunnel will simulate the effects of free falling at a speed of approximately two hundred feet per second.

With ground week completed, the students will travel to Yuma Proving Grounds, Arizona. Weeks two through five will find our candidates jumping, jumping, and jumping again, beginning at ten thousand feet with no equipment and working up to twenty-five thousand feet with full equipment load and oxygen system. The course provides in-the-air instruction where the students will concentrate on stability, aerial maneuvers, and parachute deployment procedures. Each student will receive a minimum of sixteen free-fall jumps; this will include two day and two night jumps with oxygen and full field equipment.

U.S. Air Force Survival School at Fairchild Air Force Base, Washington state, where the students will be the guests of the 336th Training Group. The mission of the school is

"To prepare America's aircrew for global survivability anytime, anywhere, and return with honor." It was to this training that U.S. Air Force Capt. Scott O'Grady credited his ability to survive on the ground after his F-16 was shot down in Bosnia.

Here in the mountains of Coville and Kanisksu national forests, approximately seventy miles north of Spokane, the cadre of the 22nd Training Squadron conducts the Combat Survival Training, basic survival techniques for remote areas. The course includes training in parachute landing falls (PLFs), life support equipment procedures, construction of a shelter, procurement of food, and its preparation. Additional survival skills will be taught, such as day and night land navigation, ground-to-air signaling, vectoring rescue aircraft to their location, and helicopter hoist training—procedures, principles, equipment, and techniques that will be needed to survive the harshness of climate and hostile environment, with minimal equipment.

Along with the survival methods, they are also given SERE (survival, escape, resistance, and evasion) training. These are methods in evasive travel, camouflage techniques, and resistance in captivity. During the SERE phase of training, students will participate in a field exercise where they will become familiar with captivity and interrogation. This training will challenge the future STS members physically, mentally, and emotionally. At the conclusion of the three weeks, they will have their debriefing and graduation.

U.S. Air Force Combat Divers School. At its location in Panama City, Florida, combat diver candidates learn to use SCUBA gear to stealthily infiltrate a target area. This training is essential to the STS teams since they are often tasked with supporting U.S. Navy SEALs and must be at home in the water, as are the frogmen.

Training will include waterborne operations both day and night. Students will be taught ocean subsurface navigation, deep diving techniques, marine hazards, and how to read tides, waves, and currents. It will be in Key West that they'll be instructed in the proper procedures of entering and exiting a submerged sub. Training in both open-circuit and closed-circuit equipment will be taught. This is not recreation diving as depths in training go down to one hundred thirty feet under diverse operating conditions.

This training phase will last six weeks. In the final week of training the students will perform an underwater compass swim. It is not sufficient to just know "how" to SCUBA dive, they must be able to execute a mission via underwater egress. Equipped with a compass board, SCUBA tank, weapon, and rucksack, they will carry out an infiltration to a point on the beach. The final week also brings more night dives, a field training exercise, and graduation.

Combat Control Team (CCT) Orientation. This two-week orientation course focuses on sports physiology, nutrition, basic exercises, combat control history, and fundamentals. During these two weeks the airman is introduced to the history of combat control, missions, and career field specific skills. Candidates are required to take part in a rigorous physical fitness program that introduces them to the type of physical training conducted during their journey through the pipeline. The course includes: running, swimming, calisthenics, weight training, team building skills, sports nutrition, sports medicine, and combat control academic and practical related skills.

Air Traffic Control School. Keesler Air Force Base, Mississippi, is where the core skill-set is attained for the potential combat controller. The candidate will be under the instruction of both civilian and U.S. Air Force air traffic controllers. This course teaches orientation into air traffic control and basic flight rules, VFR tower, radar approach control (RAPCON) procedures, aircraft recognition, aircraft performance, air navigational aids, weather, airport traffic control, flight assistance, communications, conventional approach control, and air traffic control. This is the meat and potatoes of the combat controller's task. Combat controller trainees also attend a five-day combat non-radar class. At the conclusion of this course they are prepared to take the Federal Aviation Administration's Control Tower Operator examination.

Combat Control School. Master Sgt. Paul Venturella, an instructor at the Combat Control School at Pope Air Force Base, North Carolina, relates the school's mission as, "To train United States Air Force and select joint and allied service personnel basic combat skills to support controlling air traffic in an austere combat airhead operation, [and] to provide specialized advance skills training to support combat control team leader duties, static line Jumpmaster duties, and survey operations." For the next twelve weeks and three days the school's cadre will carry out this mission with their students. Class size varies; eleven trainees per class is the average, with an optimum of twenty. The course includes combat tactics, communication and navigational equipment, land navigation, assault zone operations, air traffic control, demolitions, and fire support, and concludes with a field training exercise.

As with all branches of the service, when you hit a new school or base you go through the in-processing. For the candidates arriving at the Combat Control School it is no different. Here they are checked out in various procedures, such as CPR (cardiopulmonary resuscitation). They are issued their equipment and, like their pararescue teammates, they receive the standard ALICE field pack, size large. Unlike the PJs' medical rucksack, Master Sergeant Venturella explains, "The thing about CCT is we do so many types of missions in many different manners and configurations that it's almost impossible to list a 'standard' load." The mission dictates what the CCT will pack, he continues. "I've been on numerous real-world and training missions with rucks that can weigh as little as thirty pounds and as much as one hundred and ten pounds."

If the mission was going to be primarily air traffic control, then the controller would carry the appropriate radio setup.

Along with the radio he would carry the necessary antennas, accouterments, and extra batteries. If the team is going in to set up a runway or landing zone, they would distribute the equipment among the team. Some would carry the radios, while others would pack lights, batteries, recognition panels, and stakes to make the runway. In addition to this equipment, the CCT might include various types of electronic navigational aids, a light-gun, NVGs, or a weather kit. While certain missions do indeed determine the type of equipment, there are three items that I have never seen a CCT member without: a radio, a strobe with IR cover, and a weapon.

While at the CCT school, physical conditioning is continuously stressed. Physical training is conducted throughout the eighty-seven days of training. One day the student may be doing a six-mile run; the next day will find him performing pool work or weight training, with a rucksack march rounding out the week. This constant physical preparation ensures that future combat controllers will be up to the task, both physically and mentally for the course, field training exercise, and their assignment to a special tactics squadron.

The first two weeks of training is in tactics. In this block, the instructors impart their knowledge in small unit tactics. Students will become familiar with various weapons that will be carried on their missions. Methods of insertion from rappelling to fast roping will be taught. Team leader procedures, field hygiene, gas mask (NBC) methods, and field craft are all included in this block. At the end of the twelve weeks the students perform a tactical, static-line parachute jump for an overnight FTX that will apply the skills learned in this block.

The next block of training is communications/navigational

Combat controllers will utilize an assortment of navigational aids for air-traffic control. The VS-17 signal panel measures 72 inches by 19 inches and is colored international orange on one side and fluorescent pink on the other. Runway lights, red, green, blue, clear, and infrared can be controlled all from a small handheld device.

equipment. One of the most important tools employed by a CCT is his radio. Here the CCT will learn the practical applications that will be used in his assignment to an STS as a combat controller: radio equipment that allows ground-to-air and ground-to-ground communications; radios, such as the PRC-117F, that are useful to talk on all the radio nets (networks or frequencies), VHF, AM/FM, UHF AM/FM and SATCOM, except HF; portable radios; interteam radios; and radios mounted inside Humvees. Concurrently, communication security (COMSEC) and command and control communication will be covered in this block.

While communication is an essential tool of a CCT, it is not of much use if the aircraft has nowhere to land, or the helo has no LZ. In addition to the plethora of radio equipment, the students are exposed to a vast array of navigational aids and equipment. They will be taught how to employ the

This combat controller prepares to set up the SATCOM antennae for the PRC-117 radio. While he is getting the unit ready, other members of the team have formed a defensive perimeter and are providing security for the team.

B-2 Light gun; how to set up a runway with as little as five lights, a technique known as "Box and One"; how to use cloth panel markers, known as VS-17 panels; and how to use strobes, normal issue with IR covers to small programmable units the size of nine-volt batteries. Instruction is given on how to set up landing lights, colored as well as IR. These lights can all be controlled from a small hand unit similar to a TV remote. A practical test using all the equipment is given at the end of the class.

There will be times when the CCTs jump in with the assault force. Other times they will have to jump in with other SOFs or perhaps on their own to perform an SR or RST. On these occasions they will use the information obtained in the land navigation block at the CCT school, starting off with the basics, practical work with a map and compass, and use of the military grid reference system (MGRS). Once comfortable with these methods, they move on to GPS procedures and point-to-point navigation. As with the previous blocks, it ends with a three-day FTX, to evaluate the student's land navigation skills.

In the assault zone block they will receive practical training in the basics of establishing a drop zone, landing zone, and helicopter landing zone (HLZ). Using visual aids, they will learn how to marshal aircraft once on the ground and perform limited weather observations and assault zone management. This culminates in the establishment of an assault zone and block test.

Upon hitting the ground, the CCT may be required to remove obstacles from the tarmac to allow follow-on forces to land uninhibited. For this reason, the students go through the demolitions block. For five days they will receive knowledge and practical instruction: how to safely employ nonelectric demolitions. *Nonelectric* is defined as a timed fuse method as opposed to command detonation. Demolition techniques will be taught, including the Saddle Charge, used to cut cylindrical, mild steel targets up to 8 inches in diameter; Diamond Charge, used to cut either mild or alloy cylindrical steel of any diameter; Ribbon Charge, used to cut noncylindrical steel (that is, I beams, angle irons, and so on) up to two inches thick; and others. This culminates in practical testing in the applications, calculations, and placement of explosives.

The last block of instruction at Pope Air Force Base is fire support for four days. In the communication block the student learns how to use the radio as a tool. In this block he discovers how to transform the radio into a weapon called close air support, or CAS. Training consists of integrating CAS with ground- and sea-based weapons systems, night operations, laser procedures, mission execution, and how to call for fire interfacing with AC-130 gunships and helicopters for CAS. You only have to spend a few moments on Alpha 77 at Eglin Air Force Base to realize the awesome effect of CAS. As with the other blocks, it ends with practical evaluation of skills learned.

Now that our future combat controllers have been schooled in their trade, they are off to the Sand Hills of North Carolina, just west of Camp McKall, where the U.S. Army SF has its Q-course and SERE school. They will spend the next ten days in a comprehensive FTX applying all of the skills taught over the past twelve weeks. It begins with a mission plan, team leader brief, and equipment preparation. When they are "good to go" they will be inserted into their assigned area of operations (AO). After insertion, the students will receive various follow-on missions for the next eight days. They will be required to plan, prepare, and rehearse each mission prior to its execution. The FTX mission includes the establishment of numerous assault zones; FRIS insertion and HLZ; a run through the obstacle course (Q-course at SF Camp McKall); patrol base operations; movement of the team overland, perhaps an SR; practical exercise (equipment and procedures); and CAS knowledge employing lasing procedures using a laser designator referred to as the SOFLAM or Special Operations Force Laser Acquisition Marker. The final mission includes a border crossing back into friendly territory. On the final morning of the FTX is a 115-mile rucksack march from the field to the Combat Control School. Students are required to carry seventy pounds in their rucksack, LBE, and weapon.

Those airmen and officers completing this phase of training are qualified for assignment as combat controllers. Some will be assigned to conventional CCT in USAF Air Combat Command, while those entering AFSOC will be assigned to one of the four special tactics squadrons in the continental United States. It is at the end of this course that they are awarded the scarlet beret, with the U.S. Air Force Combat Control crest, "First There."

For the STS team member, this is just the beginning. They will go on to receive intense training in deploying the special air asset of AFSOC, including advanced training in working with "fast movers" for CAS and becoming Special Operations Tactical Air Control (SOTAC) qualified. They will undergo Ranger training and other "infantry-related" skills.

Combat controller Staff Sgt. Rick Driggers of the 720th STS maintains radio communications with orbiting MH-53E in preparation for a close air support mission. The other member of the STT carries an AN/PRC 117; multi-mission FM/AM, UHF TACSAT radio. *Staff Sgt. Rick Driggers*

Combat controllers are awarded the scarlet beret and the U.S. Air Force Combat Control crest, "First There." Upon graduation from the Pararescue School, the PJ is awarded the maroon beret with the Pararescue crest. Their motto, "That others may live," reaffirms the pararescueman's commitment to saving lives and self-sacrifice.

All of the training of the "pipeline" is essential to the success of the STS mission. It is not that they will be given the assignment to take an airfield; that would go to the Rangers. They would not be asked to fast rope onto a building and perform a hostage rescue; these operations are tasked to the SEALs or Delta Force. In each scenario, however, there will be air assets involved and possible casualties. The STS teams will be there to support such operations. This is the reason for the intensity of the "pipeline" and subsequent training. When a member of an STS team is attached to other SOF units, they must be an asset, not a liability. "The last thing you want to do is slow that SEAL team down," Master Sgt. Ron Childress (ret.) explains. "If you do . . . they will not call you in again."

Advance Skills Training Course

A decade ago combat controllers and pararescuemen went through initial familiarization (IFAM). IFAM was the gathering of PJs and CCT airmen into a cohesive unit where they are exposed to all the aspects, methods, and procedures carried out in STS operations. It was an exercise that would mold the airmen into the lethal force known as air commandos; it lasted one month.

During IFAM the PJs and CCTs, both "rookies" and experienced, would run through the paces of the "bread and butter" of STS. Ron Childress, a combat veteran CCT, related. "Here they [STS teams] find out exactly *what* we do and *how* we do it," Childress said. He and the IFAM cadre impart their knowledge, lessons learned, experience, and motivation into the up-and-coming teams that will take their place in the special tactics squadrons.

Today, those airmen going into special tactics team will attend the Advance Skills Training at Hurlburt Field, Florida. Depending on their specialty, they will add various phases of the course. The introduction of the course syllabus to the AST course reads, "Welcome to the Advanced Skills Training (AST) course, and the start of your training to become a Combat Ready special tactics Operator. AST Cadre are centered on excellence, committed to building and maintaining a consortium of joint and unilateral special operations training activities focused on the training of special operators."

The duration of the IFAM course was one month and trained approximately 14 students. In 2000 the training was tasked to decrease the time a three-level trainee would be in training to become a five level. The course has been expanded

On the ramp and ready to go, a rigged alternate method Zodiac (RAMZ) package is prepared to be deployed from a MC-130P Combat Shadow. Within seconds of the deflated Zodiac raft exiting the aircraft, the STT will follow it out. Once the team hits the water and has discarded their parachutes, they begin removing the Zodiac from the packing, inflating the raft, and getting the outboard engine, positioned, primed, and running. Once it is ready to go, they will load aboard and head for the insertion point.

to one year and encompasses all the core tasks in the combat control Career Field Education and Training Plan (CFETP), with an enrollment of more than one hundred twenty students a year. Emphasizing a hands-on approach to learning, the AST course offers the opportunity for combat control, pararescue, and combat weather trainees to interact and train in a joint team environment.

Advanced Skills Training provides the most opportune training for newly assigned special tactics operators. AST also provides STS operators the ability to become mission ready prior to joining individual STS teams. This schedule is broken down into four phases of training: Water, Ground, Employment, and Mission Qualification Training. Each of the four phases is designed to give the student the required skill to progress to the next phase. AST will push the trainee to the edge of the envelope with demanding physical as well as mental exercise. Success comes to those who are willing to give one hundred percent throughout each evolution.

Warriors Training Warriors

Using what is called the Mentoring Program, the cadre includes retired combat control senior non-commissioned officers who provide leadership, guidance, and continuity required to professionally develop and ensure the success of each student. Each of these NCO mentors brings a wealth of combat experience and extensive educational background in real-world combat controller and special tactics missions.

Phase I—Water

The mission of the water phase is to prepare special tactics operators for the Combat Diver Qualification Course (CDQC) and prepare them for the stress of waterborne operations normally encountered in the field. Students participate in extensive physical conditioning with emphasis on swimming, running, and calisthenics. This phase prepares them for the rigors of training and the demands of a battlefield airman. The first two weeks involve base and squadron in-processing. Academic training includes: dive physics, decompression dives, dive tables, dangerous marine life, and terminology. Completion of pre-SCUBA is their "ticket" to attend SCUBA School and earn the SCUBA badge. It is at the CDQC where the operator will become a combat diver and learn to use SCUBA covertly to infiltrate areas surrounded by water.

Phase II—Ground

This phase is conducted at Hurlburt Field, Florida, and Fort Bragg, North Carolina, as well as other locations. During the ninety-day Ground phase, the students will learn numerous skills that are essential to carry out their missions at combat controllers. The course syllabus describes this phase, "You will

With the four turbo-prop engines running, it is rather noisy inside of the Combat Shadow. Communications is thereby conveyed in the form of hand signals. Here, the jumpmaster for the RAMZ drop, Staff Sgt. Rick Driggers, holds up six fingers, indicating that the team is six minutes away from the insertion point. The cargo ramp will be opened and seven minutes from now the STT will be in the air.

accomplish the majority of Career Field Training Program objectives in this phase to include: command and control, Air Traffic Control, fixed and rotary wing call for fire [CFF] training, portable and vehicular communications, and demolitions. Additionally, you will become familiar with survey techniques, including AUTOCAD and global positioning systems [GPS]. You will become well versed in assault zone procedures, including actual drop zone [DZ] and landing zone [LZ] assault training missions at various locations around the continental United States."

Phase III—Employment

This phase is conducted at Hurlburt Field for a duration of ninety days. Students will be exposed to various infiltration methods of employment used by special tactics operators that include: Static line and Military Free Fall Airborne operations. Alternate insertion/extraction methods with helicopters to include fast-rope, rappel, rope ladder, and hoist operations.

During this phase students also learn military dive operations that include compass and search dive procedures. Small

Capt. Frankie Rodriquez provides some "motivational" mentoring to a 2nd Lieutenant during Advance Skills Training. The captain is a master in the art of war and a veteran of multiple incursions into enemy territory in support of OEF. He, as well as other members of the cadre, is more than capable of providing the students with the necessary guidance to facilitate their evolution into battlefield airmen. *U.S. Air Force*

boat operations include preparation for employment; capsize drills, intercostals, riverine, and navigation. Small unit tactics skills are sharpened with weapons, dismounted patrols, and tactical vehicle operations. As in the other two previous phases of instruction, PT will consist of full battle dress uniform, LBE, weapon, swimming, running, ruck marches, trail runs, and an obstacle course.

Phase IV—Mission Qualification Training

The shortest phase of AST is the MQT coming in at seventy days. Here students learn the skills regarding mission planning, including various types of orders, planning considerations, ST Intel support capabilities, and use of Falcon View mission planning software. They will use this planning process during every full mission profile (FMP).

The students receive a mission frag order and plan and prepare for a three-day FMP. The profiles will include a Helo Soft-Duck insertion, overland movement, target recon, and exfiltration to friendly lines. Students develop recall procedures and assume an alert posture with a thirty-minute response time.

These future battlefield airmen will travel to Sandrock, Alabama, where they learn military mountaineering techniques to include: basic securing/hauling systems, stokes litter, single man pick-offs, rappelling, bouldering, and rock-climbing skills.

Students also receive classes on the history, purpose, and detailed planning consideration required to successfully execute a full-blown airfield seizure. They will be taught how to build bike-bundle packages and conduct a day Jump Clearing Team operation. In addition to the day work, they will perform a night airfield seizure; FMP is conducted, including more than a half dozen fixed and rotary wing aircraft at OLF Choctaw, Florida, or Tonopah Test Range, Nevada. The exercise is followed by a detailed aircrew/instructor debrief.

Graduation

Upon completing all four phases of AST, graduating the Combat Diver Course, Military Free Fall Parachutist Course, and passing the two Career Development Courses, the operators are now ready to become a combat control journeyman. Their mission will be as a highly trained weapon system and force multiplier, ready to deploy.

Pararescue Indoctrination Course

The journey for a slot at a PJ in the special tactics squadrons begins in the hot Texas sun, near San Antonio, at Lackland Air Force Base. For twelve grueling weeks potential team members go through the Pararescue Indoctrination Course. Here, the volunteers show whether they have what it takes to enter into the highly selective, extremely aggressive, and high-risk world of Air Force Special Operations.

The Indoc course selects, screens, and trains the potential PJs for their specialty field. The candidate is at the threshold of a year's journey through some of the military's most intensive training. Indoctrination is designed to push the students mentally and physically to their limits and beyond. This training prepares them for the high standards they will be expected to meet as they make their way through the pipeline and their ultimate assignment—combat. During Indoc the instructors will place the students in highly stressful situations that will challenge their mental capabilities, their physical qualities, and most important, their determination and perseverance to stick it out until the job is done. There is no room in STS or any other SOF unit for an individual who wants to quit when things get rough. Students who graduate from the Indoctrination Course will have developed the skills that should prevent them from failure in the pipeline if they give and maintain one hundred percent dedication.

For the next twelve weeks the candidates will hone themselves to a mental and physical razor's edge. Run training consists of long, slow distances, sprints, interval training, and others. The pace for evaluation is a seven-minute mile. Weight training programs are included to develop strength, endurance, and speed. Interspersed between these activities comes calisthenics, assorted, at the judgment of the instructors.

In week three the trainees experience "Motivation Week" or "Hell Week"—actually, three days, but it seems like a week, and one that is never going to end. One moment our trainees are resting in their bunks and the next moment they are belly down, face in the dirt, crawling under barbed wire through the obstacle course. The exercise goes on nonstop: no sleep, pushing the envelope of their inner strength. Motivation Week separates the overwhelmed from the serious operators. Hell Week cuts the class size; it is not unheard of that out of a class of eighty, nine volunteers graduate.

From day one and throughout IC, the candidates will find themselves in the water. Here the candidates are subjected to water confidence and swim training. This is the same training that the officer students were exposed to in Phase II. At indoctrination, the enlisted get their feet wet, literally, as they learn underwater swimming; fin swimming; mask and snorkel recovery; buddy breathing/pool harassment; bobbing; underwater knots; ditch and donning equipment; treading water; weight belt swim; and the ever-popular drownproofing. For the officer trainees, they get to appreciate this course a second time; practice does make perfect!

The course also will concentrate on marksmanship training (M-16A1 rifle and M-9 pistol), physiological training (altitude and dive chambers), as well as academic instruction in dive physics and metric measurements. Upon graduation from this selection process, the airmen and officers now have their ticket to ride the pipeline, and they will move on to numerous military specialty schools.

Pararescue School

PJ Medical training and Rescue training is conducted at Kirtland Air Force Base, New Mexico.

Emergency Medical Technician Basic and Paramedic Courses: The Emergency Medical Training consists of the EMT-Basic and EMT-Paramedic Courses running concurrently for all enlisted pipeline students. All students must successfully complete all portions of the EMT-B course, before entering the EMT-P course. All students MUST successfully complete each program and obtain National Registry certification prior to attending the PJ Apprentice course.

EMT-Basic Training: The course is twenty-three days, one hundred eighty-seven hours in duration. The performance and didactic portions comply with the Department of Transportations National Standard Curriculum. The course curriculum provides basic knowledge and skills in emergency, pre-hospital care necessary for entrance into the EMT-P course. The program teaches: Anatomy and Physiology with cadaver lab at UNM, Assessment/Care of the Trauma patient, Assessment/Care of the Medical Patient, Assessment/Care of the Pediatric patient, Assessment/Care of the Geriatric patient, HAZMAT, and Identification and treatment of Environmental injuries.

EMT-Paramedic Training: The course is a one hundred seventeen days, one thousand, two hundred hours in duration. The performance and didactic portions comply with the Department of Transportation's National Standard Curriculum. Course curriculum builds on and reinforces the basic knowledge/skills previously learned in EMT-B while focusing on advanced emergency procedures and techniques. The program focuses on advanced airway management, advanced shock management/intravenous therapy, pharmacology/medication administration, cardiology, pre-hospital trauma life support, advanced cardiac life support, pediatric advanced life support, advanced surgical skills/suturing, mass casualty/triage, and diseases of military importance. The program also requires students to complete a six-week clinical/field training. Students are assigned to medical treatment facilities and emergency medical pre-hospital care agencies. Students MUST successfully complete this phase of training and obtain the recommendation from their clinical preceptor in order to test for National Registry certification.

Upon graduation of the Medical training, the candidate is certified as an Emergency Medical Technician-Paramedic. Having received their certification as an EMT-P they continue to the PJ rescue training. The Pararescue Recovery Specialist Course, the final course, which is uniquely tailored for pararescuemen, is divided into three phases: ground, air, and medical.

The future PJ receives quite extensive training and with good reason. A U.S. Army medic in the Rangers, for example, is schooled in advanced combat medicine. He is fully capable of providing first aid treatment to his company during a mission. The medical specialists on a U.S. Army Special Forces A-team are also highly trained. According to Carol Darby of the USASOC PAO, "Some SF medical sergeants who obtain the MOS of 18D can be as qualified as many physician assistants, maybe more." Although capable of providing combat medicine, their missions more often revolve around organizing medical care in civic actions, humanitarian operations, preventative medicine, and care of the A-team members and indigenous guerrilla forces in unconventional warfare operations.

For pararescuemen assigned to AFSOC, though capable, their mission is not to perform fundamental first aid or civic actions. Special tactics squadron PJs do not have the comfort of working out of an aid station or having a Black Hawk sitting 10 yards away leisurely waiting for them. They have to get to the casualty, evaluate, stabilize, and extract, most likely while under hostile fire. Air Force Special Operations PJs are proficient medical specialists who are fully trained as dive medics and excel in the science of trauma medicine.

The U.S. Air Force major commands have determined what qualifications pararescuemen must possess for assignment to their commands. Air Combat Command looks for an emergency medical technician-intermediate, while Air Force Special Operations Command requires its personnel to obtain the emergency medical technician-paramedic qualification. Medical training at Kirtland is specially designed to meet the U.S. Air Force requirements. Drive-along programs are included in the training regime. The PJs will accompany emergency rescue ambulance crews in various major cities. They will see the lacerations and punctures created by knife wounds, the blast and cavitations from gun shots, and fractures and crushing wounds found in vehicular accidents; in other words, trauma medicine.

Ground Phase

The student will be taught fieldcraft, firecraft, woodcraft, and accelerated survival techniques. Although the probability is rare, a PJ may be placed in a survival situation, on his own or with a wounded individual, perhaps a downed pilot. Trainees will learn how to live "off the land." Instruction will be given in identifying edible plants and how to obtain and prepare food from various wilderness sources. Master Stg. Rick Weaver, an instructor at the Pararescue School, explains, "They [the students] have learned how to survive during the U.S. Air Force survival course. Now we want to see what they've learned. How do you start a fire? Show me how you get water from a pine branch by placing a plastic bag over it and squeezing off the moisture."

There may be times, for whatever reasons, that a PJ may be stuck on the ground alone. For this reason, PJs are taught field operations and tactics at Kirtland. They are instructed in how to evade capture in enemy territory and how to survive. This exercise is a point-to-point movement; the student must locate and extract a casualty. While doing so, the school's cadre will be out looking for those in the field. The difference between this and the survival school is the evasion and escape exercises are not as intense at Kirtland. The cadre does not hunt you down and take you prisoner. It is designed to instill a confident outlook and positive attitude, to accept the circumstances, and "drive-on" at all cost.

Part of the ground phase includes lessons in navigation. Each candidate is required to be proficient in daylight or nighttime navigation. He must know the basics of geography, how to read a map and navigate from one, and how to use a compass, a pace counter, and altimeter to determine his exact location. "The primary method of navigation," outlined by Master Sgt. Weaver, "are the stars, lensatic compass, any compass, and a map. They must learn the basics." The global positioning system is taught, but it is used as a secondary method. However, as Weaver depicts, ". . . If you use it [GPS] all the time it will become a crutch." There are times when batteries go dead or the unit is not available. The student is expected to accomplish these skills in the darkest night with and without the aid of night-vision goggles (NVGs). The trainee will be evaluated on his navigational prowess during a ten-day navigational exercise in a mountainous environment; well suited for such an exercise is the Manzano Mountains just south of Albuquerque, New Mexico.

While on the subject of mountains, the students will learn how to traverse, climb over, and rappel down a mountain. This may be done alone or with a casualty. During this phase of training they will become familiar with various mountaineering equipment, such as carabiners, chokes, ice axes, and so on. They will learn to tie more knots than a Boy Scout and how to work with ropes to build rope bridges. From belaying techniques to mountain walking, the trainees will become one with the mountain. Since mountains, as the sea, are unforgiving, it is this training that will result in a successful rescue, or the loss of a survivor and perhaps the rescue team.

The mountaineering instruction begins with "The Tower," a climbing and abseiling, or rappelling, structure forty feet high. Here the students are given ample time to practice their climbing skills. The tower is arrayed with various "rocks" that lead to the top of it. This simulates climbing the mountain. The student must accomplish this task without the aid of sophisticated commercial mountaineering equipment. Once the climbing skills are accomplished, the instructors break out the latest "high-speed" climbing equipment for the trainees to learn. One might ask, why not bring out all this high-tech climbing gear right from the start? It is like learning long division; first you must know the basics, then you learn the short cuts. Pararescuemen have to accomplish their mission. Sometimes that includes using the latest mountaineering gear; other times, it means using their hands, arms, legs, and brains to complete the rescue.

As the trainees learn that what goes up must come down, they will learn the proper techniques in rappelling. How to rappel down the side of a mountain with a 90-pound rucksack or how to abseil down the side of a cliff with a wounded pilot in a stokes litter. They will also learn how to belay another climber down the face of the mountain.

Upon completion of the classroom work and the practicing on the tower, the candidates head out to the Pecos Mountains. Here for the next ten days they will carry out field and mountain operations. Upon arrival to the base of the mountain, they will establish a base camp from where operations will be carried out. There, instructors will give them further training in fieldcraft and land search.

For the next four mornings they will head to the mountain for actual practice on the rocks. They rehearse basic rock climbing, ascending, rappelling, litter evacuations, river crossing, and improvised mountaineering setups. On the final day the instructors will evaluate all the trainees on every aspect of mountaineering. Students must pass all of these evaluations before they are allowed to continue the field training exercise.

The next five days of the operation will find the trainees practicing navigation and adverse terrain movement techniques as they traverse the mountain in planned routes. They will move from location to location and must become proficient in establishing their coordinates on a map. Students are required to ascertain their position within 50 meters at any time. This is to be done without the aid of a GPS unit. As the future PJs move along they will have more opportunities to practice fieldcraft skills. They will set up a camp, build a fire, forage for food, and be tasked with exercises ranging from building a rope bridge to treating a simulated casualty—all under the watchful eyes of their instructors. At the end of these five days they will be evaluated; those who pass move on to the next phase of training—Tactics.

STS teams, like other Special Operations forces, often operate in small groups, so they must learn small unit tactics. During the pararescue course this subject will be infused into the skills of the PJ. They will learn how to operate as a small team under extreme conditions. In addition, they will learn how to interface with other operators, such as SEALs, Rangers, Special Forces, and Special Air Service forces for quick integration.

While in this phase of training the students will be run through various scenarios and exercises planned by their instructors with an emphasis on night operations. A test of the small team unit integrity will come when the students face their instructors operating as an "OpForce." Will the team hold together, or will they break and run? You cannot have a quitter in a special tactics squadron.

Ninety percent of the training mission will be performed at night. Some will use night-vision goggles or devices extensively, while others will not. The trainees must learn how to operate with and without the aid of high-tech gear. This will teach them the benefits as well as the limitations of each scenario. Students are also instructed in the tactics of a nuclear, biological, and chemical (NBC) battlefield environment.

At the end of the Tactics phase of training, the candidates are sent on a three- to five-day tactical mission. This mission will test their skills in reaching their objective, perhaps a survivor, treating the casualty, preparing them to be moved, and evacuation.

All trainees will become familiar with various types of signaling and communications. They will learn how to improvise signals such as creating a signal out of wood or cloth panels. They will also receive training with the more sophisticated

survival and long-range radios. Communications is one of the most essential tools in the PJs' selection of mission equipment.

Medical Phase

Individuals in the PJ career path are issued the standard all-purpose light individual carrying equipment (ALICE) field pack, size large. This is the same ruck found among SF A-teams, Rangers, and fellow CCTs; the difference is that the PJ's ruck is replete with medical supplies. It's filled to the brim with a first aid kit, space blanket, surgical kit, tracheotomy kit, bandaging, IV infusor kit, diagnostic kit, poleless litter, assorted splints, stethoscope, medications, and so on. Each PJ's medical rucksack is arranged exactly the same, in the event a PJ would have to work out of another team member's pack. For example, the lower three large pockets on

A pararescue sergeant administers an IV to a wounded team member. Pararescuemen, also known as parajumpers (PJs), are highly trained in dealing with the numerous types of injuries they may encounter. They are also trained in the latest methods of trauma medicine. From simple procedures to the treatment of gunshot wounds the pararescuemen are tops in their fields.

the outside of the rucksack are designated A, B, and C for *airway*, *bleeding*, and *circulation*. If any member of the team requires a battle dressing, he would know to go directly to the B, or lower, middle pocket. Other specialized medical equipment may be issued or transported with the STS team, dictated by mission parameters.

Team members will learn how to set up and properly wear their LBE (load-bearing equipment) and ALICE packs. It will not be uncommon for the medical rucks to weigh ninety or more pounds and the LBE to carry more than twenty pounds of gear. They will learn how to pack this gear and carry it as comfortably as possible. The PJs must learn how to move efficiently and stealthily under their load. They will have to learn how to navigate through an aircraft fuselage as well as through a wooded terrain or mountain slope.

Students will learn techniques and procedures on the use of the rapid extraction deployment system (REDS). Similar to the "jaws of life" found on fire trucks around the country, the REDS is used to cut away an aircraft fuselage to extricate

A pararescueman uses the rapid extrication device system (REDS) on a downed helicopter to aid in the extraction of the pilot from the aircraft. Similar to the "jaws-of-life" carried by various fire departments, this equipment can cut and chew its way through metal, wires, and airframe to get to a crew member.

a casualty. The REDS kit will contain a generator, combo tool, axes, reciprocal saw, and other necessary hardware to aid in the removal of the injured personnel. Students will also learn how to rig the REDS for fast rope.

While at Kirtland, the class will be taught how to conduct an actual search, from beginning the mission planning and implementation to the complete rescue and exfiltration. Using the information from their class, they will form into a rescue team, determine how to set up a base camp, and execute the mission of locating, treating, and evacuating a survivor.

Air Phase

The final phase of the Pararescue and Recovery Course is Air Operations. Here, the trainees will become familiar with aircraft and aircrew knowledge: how to perform an aerial search pattern, emergency procedures, and various aircraft systems operations. The trainees will be taught alternate insertion/extraction (AIE) methods. Helicopter techniques such as rope ladders, hoists, rappelling, and fast roping (from thirty to one hundred twenty feet) are all taught in this segment of training. The students will also learn how to helocast from helicopters. This entails deploying into the water from an altitude of approximately ten feet at a rough speed of ten knots.

Advanced parachuting techniques are taught in this phase. Students will learn how to waterproof and rig their equipment with SCUBA tanks. Pararescuemen will be introduced to the "tree suit," officially called the parachutist rough terrain system (PRTS). This is a specially manufactured suit having extra padding to protect the neck, armpits, kidneys, elbows, crotch, and knees of the jumper. It was designed for the purpose of jumping into heavily wooded environments and has a large pocket to stow up to fifty feet of rope to facilitate lowering the jumper to the ground should the parachutist get hung up in a tree. Each trainee will make ten land jumps, two tree jumps, and five SCUBA jumps, totaling seventeen, of which four to six will be night jumps.

Upon completion of this course, the qualified airman is ready for assignment to any pararescue unit worldwide. Those who complete the pararescue training are awarded the maroon beret and wear the U.S. Air Force crest, "That Others May Live."

Chapter 7

SPECIAL OPERATIONS TECHNIQUES

There are times when a team cannot just drop into an enemy's backyard, for political reasons, or strategic or tactical considerations. You must insert your team clandestinely from afar and outside of the nation's territorial airspace or boundaries. For such an insertion a U.S. Special Operations team would use either high altitude low opening (HALO) or high altitude high opening (HAHO). Both of these methods are common among U.S. Navy SEALs and Army Special Forces A-teams. For that reason, the AFSOC STS teams will also learn and become proficient in performing these procedures alongside their U.S. Army and Navy SOF operators.

These types of parachute operations will be flights over or adjacent to the objective area from altitudes not normally associated with conventional static-line parachuting. HALO/HAHO infiltrations are normally conducted under the cover of darkness or at twilight to lessen the chance of observation by hostile forces. Using the RAPS, the STS teams deploy their parachutes at a designated altitude, assemble in the air, and land together in the arranged drop zone to begin their mission. This type of drop can be conducted even in adverse weather conditions.

Flying at an altitude of twenty-five thousand to forty-three thousand feet MSL (mean sea level), a Combat Talon will appear as legitimate aircraft on an enemy's radar screen, perhaps just another commercial airliner traversing the globe. What the radar operator will not know is that the aircraft is the launching platform for the world's most lethal system, a detachment of highly trained U.S. Army Special Forces, "shooters" with their assigned STS team attached.

Military free fall operations (MFF) are ideally adapted for the infiltration of STS and SOF personnel. While the maximum exit altitude is forty-three thousand feet MSL, MFF operations may be as low as five thousand feet above ground level (AGL). A typical STS team can be deployed in the fraction of the time it would take a conventional static-line jump. Normal opening altitudes range from three thousand, five hundred AGL to twenty-five thousand MSL, depending on mission parameters.

As the AFSOC pilots approach the insertion point, the ramp of the MC-130H will lower. With the combination of aircraft noise and wearing the MFF parachutist helmet and oxygen mask, any type of verbal communication is almost impossible. For this reason the team will communicate with arm-and-hand signals. Having already received the signals to don helmets, unfasten seat belts, and check oxygen, the jumpmaster waits for the team to signal back "OK." Further instruction will be given to the jumpers as to wind speed and any gusting, all using silent signaling.

Approximately two minutes before the insertion, the jumpmaster raises his arm upward from his side indicating the team should "stand up." Next he extends his arm straight out at shoulder level, palm up, then bends it to touch his helmet, this indicating "move to the rear." The special tactics team members, equipped with ram-air parachutes, oxygen masks, and goggles, stand up and get ready to jump. If jumping from the side jump door, he'll be a meter away; if going out the rear of the plane, the lead man will stop at the hinge of the cargo ramp. With their rucksacks filled with mission-essential equipment, they waddle toward the rear of the plane.

Left: An STS combat controller fast ropes out of an MH-53E. For this trip his team will exit the starboard door of the helicopter. The "fast rope" may also be attached in the rear of the aircraft and the special operations troops would exit off the rear cargo ramp. The proper procedure is to swing out so your rucksack does not get caught on the airframe and hang you up. This CCT member is properly positioned and on his way to a fast slide to the ground. Carrying an AN/PRC 117 radio he will be ready to set up for close air support upon hitting the ground. Once the team has completed the "fast rope," the Pave Low gunner will release the latch and the heavy woolen rope drops to the ground. Depending on the mission parameters, the rope may be dropped or may be dragged back into the helicopter so no telltale signs are left of the STT insertion.

Moments turn into an eternity, and then it is time; as the aircraft reaches the proper coordinates for the drop, the jump light emits a steady green. The command is given, "Go!" In a matter of seconds the team of Air Commandos, looking like a giant centipede, shuffles down the ramp and out into the darkness as the drone of the plane's engines fades off in the distance.

Depending on the mission parameters, they will perform a HALO or HAHO jump. In HALO, the team will exit the plan and free fall through the airspace, meeting up at a pre-arranged time or altitude. Jumping in this manner, the team is so small that they are virtually invisible and, of course, will not show up on any enemy radar screen. Using GPS units and

altimeters, the team will descend until fairly close to the drop zone. At that point they will open their chutes and prepare for the very short trip to the ground.

The alternate method HAHO is also jumping from an extreme height with oxygen. The difference is that as soon as the team jumps off, they immediately deploy their parachutes and use them to glide into a denied area. For this type of jump, they would also use GPS units and altimeters. To maintain formation integrity, each jumper would have a strobe on his helmet, either normal or IR, and the team would wear the appropriate NVGs. Additionally, each team member would be on interteam radio for command and control of the insertion, as well as formation on the DZ.

The fast rope is made from eight stands of nylon synthetic line, which is designed to facilitate the insertion of personnel from a hovering helicopter. The rope is approximately two inches in diameter providing ease of handling, a sure grip, and a minimum stretch. The rope comes in fifty- to one-hundred-twenty-foot lengths, allowing the special tactics teams to insert onto various structures and environments. Also shown here is a pair of standard issue rappelling gloves (tan) and a pair of HellStorm heavy-duty fast rope gloves (black) from Black Hawk Industries. The gloves incorporate a heat barrier palm pad to protect the wearers as they insert. The glove also has a quick release wrist cinch and a carabineer loop to attach the gloves to an assault vest or LBE.

There are a number of advantages of using the HALO/HAHO procedures. There are times when the presence of enemy air defenses makes it best to infiltrate a team into a hostile area. This also increases the survivability of the support aircraft. If the mission requires the team to jump into a mountainous terrain where it would not be practical or prudent to attempt a static-line parachute operation, MFF would be a practical option. Other benefits include times when navigational aids (NAVAIDS) are not available to guarantee the requisite precision of drops at low altitudes (i.e., deserts or jungle environments), or when it is deemed necessary to land the team at multiple points of an objective for the purpose of attacking or seizing a primary target and the mission success requires a low-signature infiltration.

FRIS

The fast rope insertion system (FRIS) is the new way to get your assault force on the ground in seconds. This system begins with small, woven wool ropes that are braided into a larger rope. The rope is rolled into a deployment bag and the end is secured to the helicopter. Depending on the model of chopper, it can be just outside on the hoist mechanism or attached to a bracket off the back ramp. Once over the insertion point the rope is deployed, and even as it is hitting the ground the STS team members are jumping onto it and sliding down, as easily as a firefighter goes down a pole. Once the team is safely on the ground, the gunner or flight engineer on the helicopter will pull the safety pin, and the rope will fall to the ground. Such a system is extremely useful in the rapid deployment of special tactics squadrons personnel, as well as the other Special Operations forces that have mastered the technique. Unlike rappelling, once the trooper hits the ground, he is "free" of the rope and can begin his mission.

SPIES

While fast roping gets you down quick, there are times when you have to get out of Dodge just as fast. The problem is, there is no LZ for the MH-53E Pave Low to land, and the bad guys are closing in on your position. This technique began during the Vietnam War as the McGuire rig, then it

was modified to the STABO rig. Both used multiple ropes, which often resulted in the troops colliding into one another; the latter at least had the benefit of allowing the user to use his weapon while on the ride up. What served the Special Forces troops of the 1960s has been refined to the new special procedure insertion extraction system (SPIES) method.

While the technique has changed, the methodology remains. A *single* rope is lowered from the hovering helicopter. Attached to this rope are rings, woven and secured into the rope at approximately five-foot intervals. There can be as many as eight rings on the rope. The STS team members, wearing special harnesses similar to parachute harnesses, will attach themselves to the rope, via the rings. This is accomplished by clipping in a snap link that is at the top of the harness.

Once all team members are secured, a signal is given and the STS team becomes airborne in reverse and extracted out of harm's way. While tried and tested, this method allows the team to maintain covering fire from their weapons as they extract.

Once the STS team has been rushed out of enemy range and an LZ can be located, the helicopter pilot will bring the troops to ground again. At this time they will disconnect from the rope and board the chopper, which will then finish the extraction.

SPIES is not without risks, as the pilot of the helicopter must take care not to drag the commandos through the trees or other permanent ground fixtures, such as rocks, mountain sides, or buildings. The AFSOC helicopter pilots are remarkably proficient at seeing this does not happen.

Rappelling

With fast rope insertion system (FRIS) being the most accepted way of getting a force onto the ground expeditiously, there are still occasions when STS teams will use rappelling to accomplish their mission. There are times when working in a mountainous terrain, or in an urban environment, that this technique will come in handy.

Attaching regular military-issue rope through carabiners, or a specially designed rappelling device (known as a "Figure 8"), the team will negotiate down the side of a mountain to reach a downed pilot or establish an observation point for SR.

This old mountaineering technique has served Special Forces troops for decades and is still a viable asset in the inventory of skills of the special tactics squadrons.

Rubber Duck

A "rubber duck" is the term SOF troops will use to describe a mission where there is a need to deploy a Zodiac raft. There are numerous methods of conveying the craft to the water, and the AFSOC aircrews and STS teams are specialists at all of them.

There is the "soft duck." Here, the fully inflated Zodiac raft is deployed from the rear cargo ramp of an MH-53 Pave Low or an MH-47 Chinook. The raft is slid out of the helicopter and the STT follows right behind. Once in the water, the team jumps in, fires up the outboard engine, and heads out on the mission. An alternate to this is the *hard duck;* this is a craft with a metal bottom, and it is delivered in the same manner as the soft duck.

Another method of deployment is the K duck; the "k" stands for "kangaroo." As the name implies, the Zodiac raft is slung underneath a Pave Hawk. It is fully inflated and mission ready upon hitting the water. Rounding out the alphabet ducks is the "t duck"; the "t" stands for "tether." In this case the raft is totally deflated, rolled up, and secured inside the helicopter. Once deployed, as before, the team will inflate, load up, and begin its mission.

Two fully inflated Zodiac rafts are palletized, rigged, and await loading onto an AFSOC aircraft. Among the load will be the engines that will be set in place once they hit the water and have been separated. The STT will then enter the raft and begin their over-water insertion.

Moving from the rotary to the fixed-wing methods, there is the *RAMZ* drop. Pronounced "rams," it is defined as a rigging alternate method–Zodiac. Originally designed by the PJs for NASA shuttle missions, the Zodiac raft is fully deflated and secured to a disposable pallet; parachutes are then attached to the harness, securing the package. Moments after the loadmaster releases the package, the STS troops will shuffle to the end of the ramp and parachute in after it. A variation of the deflated method is the *double duck*, where two Zodiacs, fully inflated, are stacked and deployed via parachute together. Both the RAMZ and Double would be delivered by a Combat Talon or Combat Shadow.

The STS members are capable of inserting by land, air, and in this case, sea. This scout swimmer of the STT arrives on the beach; he'll pause at the water's edge. Keeping his rifle up and ready, he will survey the surroundings and bring the rest of the team up on his signal.

Chapter 8

WEAPONS AND EQUIPMENT

Pistols

In 1985, the U.S. military adopted the Beretta Model 92F 9mm semiautomatic pistol as the standard-issue sidearm for U.S. troops Along with the standardization of the 9mm, the M9 brought the armed forces a larger-capacity magazine. The M9 holds fifteen rounds compared to the Colt 1911's seven or eight rounds. Although the 9mm ammunition was lighter and smaller, it was viewed that this was adequate for line troops. This trade-off also allowed the troops to engage more rounds in a firefight before needing to reload.

The M9 features a rotating firing pin system with decocking and trigger bar disconnect. A magazine release is positioned at the base of the trigger guard, accommodating either left-handed or right-handed shooters. The slide is open for nearly the entire length of the barrel. This facilitates the ejection of spent shells and virtually eliminates stoppages. The open slide configuration also provides a means for the pistol to be loaded manually.

As with all weapons in use with Special Operations forces, the operators are always trying to get that extra edge. One of the most likely features to be added to the M9 was a sound suppressor. For such a device the military turned to Knight Armament Company to produce the needed suppressor. The smooth, cylindrical suppressor is made of anodized aluminum with a steel attachment system. Weighing a scant 6 ounces, it can be replaced or removed in three seconds. Carrying over the Vietnam-era name, the suppressor was dubbed the "Hush-Puppy."

Joint SOF Combat Pistol Program

While the U.S. military may have switched to the M9 Beretta, it was never accepted nor adopted by the door-kickers as a serious weapon, especially for counter terrorism and hostage rescue missions. The Joint SOF Combat Pistol program is being conducted by SOCOM to evaluate the future handgun for U.S. SOF units—caliber 45! Currently in the preliminary stages of development, the program will be examining the offerings of several manufacturers. Among the weapons being considered by SOCOM is the HK45 manufactured by Heckler & Koch.

The HK45 is based on their universal self-loading pistol. Following the USP design, the HK45 has ambidextrous slide and magazine releases. The polygonal barrel and linkless operating system are housed in a steel slide that is mated to a polymer frame. Depending on the operator's preference, the weapon can be configured for single action (SA), double action (DA), or double action only (DAO). To accommodate various users, the hand-grip features interchangeable backstraps. Molded into the frame is a Mil Std 1913 rail permitting the attachment of lasers, lights, etc. The HK45 comes in two models; the full size HK45 and the compact HK45C. Both of the handguns can be fitted with threaded barrels to facilitate the attachment of a suppressor. While other companies are being considered, the HK45 certainly looks like the pick of the litter.

Stealth and secrecy can best be maintained with the help of a suppressed weapon. Here, a combat controller uses a M9 Beretta fitted with a suppressor.

Left: The M9 is a lightweight, semiautomatic pistol manufactured by Beretta, which replaced the 1911A1 in the mid-eighties as the standard issue sidearm. It can be fired as either a double- or single-action and is chambered for 9mm NATO ammunition. The weapon is lighter than the 1911 and carries almost twice the ammunition, fifteen rounds versus eight. The ammunition is in a double-stack format, which does make the grip of the pistol wider than the 1911.

HK Submachine Guns
MP5

Although U.S. Special Operations forces have transitioned to the M4A1 carbine as their primary weapon, you can still find the German-made Heckler & Koch MP5 sub-machine gun in their armories. There are operators in the community who believe the MP5 still has a viable place in CT, CQB, and personal protection operations. One special tactics officer

The U.S. military has finally come to the table and realized the .45 caliber pistol is "the" caliber of choice for real-world operations. One of the top competitors for the replacement of the venerable 1911 is Heckler and Koch. Seen here are four versions of the proposed CPS. Starting clockwise from the upper left is the HK45, HK45 tactical, the HK45 compact tactical with suppressor, and the HK45 compact with magazine extension. As this book goes to print the SOF pistol program has been placed on hold. However, as GWOT continues, it is very likely these pistols will find their way into the hands of operators down range. *Heckler and Koch photo*

comments, ". . . (T)he MP5 still has its place; the SD model is especially useful in sentry removal." The MP5 family of submachine guns is simple to handle as well as fast and accurate, whether firing from the shoulder or the hip.

The MP5 employs the same delayed blowback operated roller-locked bolt system found in the proven HK G3 automatic rifle. All the characteristics of HK, reliability, ease of handling, simple maintenance, and safety, are accentuated on the MP5. Firing from the closed-bolt position during all modes of fire makes MP5 submachine guns extremely accurate and controllable. Its high accuracy results form the fixed barrel, which is cold forged together with the cartridge chamber. The recoil of the MP5 is extremely smooth allowing the shooter to obtain highly accurate shot placement. It fires a 9mm Parabellum pistol round usually carried in a thirty-round magazine, and is often equipped with a dual magazine holder. An operator with an MP5 can be very effective when encountering a terrorist in a hostage situation or when engaging other mission critical targets.

Common throughout each of the MP5 series of weapons is the capability to use various interchangeable assemblies and components. This provides the ability for operators to train with one weapon group and have them competent with the entire weapon system. The series also includes an accessory claw-lock scope mount and telescopic sight. HK scope mounts as wells as others, such as ARMS mounts, attach to the weapons without any special tools at special points that ensure one hundred percent return to zero.

MP5N

The MP5N was developed by HK especially for the U.S. Navy SEALs. The MP5 "Navy" model comes standard with an ambidextrous trigger group and threaded barrel. The MP5-N fires from a closed and locked bolt in either the semiautomatic or automatic modes. This sub-gun is recoil operated and has a

There is nothing that has the feel of a Heckler and Koch MP5, 9mm submachine gun. Once the weapon of choice for many Special Operations forces and the preferred weapon for close quarters battle (CQB), it has all but been replaced by the M4A1 carbine. Nevertheless, you can still find the submachine gun "Down Range" in service with SOCOM units. As a member of the blue team of the 720th STS stated, "HK—the easy way out!"

unique delayed roller locked bolt system, a retractable butt stock, a removable suppressor, and illuminating flashlight integral to the forward hand guard. The flashlight is operated by a pressure switch custom fitted to the pistol grip. The basic configuration of this weapon makes for an ideal size, weight, and capable close quarters battle weapon system.

MP5SD

For missions where stealth and secrecy is paramount, requiring fully integrated sound and flash suppression, the operators may turn to the HK MP5SD models. The model type, SD comes from the German term for "sound dampened" or Schalldampfer. The removable sound suppressor is integrated into the MP5's design and measures up to the normal length and profile of a standard, unsuppressed submachine gun. The

There are times when you need to enter with only a whisper. For those occasions, the STT will utilize the MP5-SD3. This is the same type of submachine gun as the MP5, but is fitted with an integral sound suppressor. The most noise comes from the action of the bolt as it chambers and ejects 9mm rounds.

An STT CSAR team poses with their aircraft during OIF. Each operator is equipped with a version of the Colt M4A1, which they have personalized with various accessories from the Special Operations peculiar modification (SOPMOD) accessory kit. The M4A1 features a collapsible stock, a flat top upper receiver with an accessory rail, and a detachable handle/rear aperture sight assembly. The rail interface system, or RIS, allows the attachment of numerous aiming devices and accessories depending on the mission. A variety of accessories include the EOTech HDS and Aimpoint Comp-ML optical sights and AN/PEQ-2. Attached to three of the weapons is a quick attach/detach (QAD) sound suppressor. With the suppressor attached the muzzle blast, flash, and sound are significantly reduced. *U.S. Air Force*

This combat control has mounted the Trijicon ACOG advanced combat optical gunsight atop his M4A1. The ACOG is a four power telescopic sight including a ballistic compensating reticle. Utilizing this reticle provides increased capability to direct, identify, and hit a target to the maximum effective range of the M4A1 carbine out to six hundred meters. Attached to the RIS are SOPMOD items, including a Surefire Millennium M900A vertical foregrip weapon light, an AN/PEQ-2, and attached to the barrel the QD suppressor. Additionally, the weapon has been fitted with the Crane stock, and a MagpulTM on the 30-round magazine. *U.S. Air Force*

MP5SD uses an integral aluminum or optional wet technology stainless steel sound suppressor. It does not require use of subsonic ammunition for effective sound reduction as do most conventional sound suppressed submachine guns. The MP5SD3 has an S-E-F trigger group and the MP5SD6 has a three-round burst group.

M4A1 carbine

The Colt M4A1 carbine is the standard issue weapon for special tactics teams. The M4A1 is a smaller, compact version of the full-sized M16A2 rifle. The main deference between the standard M4 and the M4A1 is the fire selector for the M4 can be selected for semi or three-round burst, while the M4A1 has a fire selection for semi- and full-automatic operation. The M4A1 is designed for speed of action and lightweight requirements as is often the case for the battlefield airman. The barrel has been redesigned to a shortened 14.5 inches, which reduces the weight, while maintaining its effectiveness for quick handling field operations. The retractable butt stock has four intermediate stops allowing versatility in CQB without compromising shooting capabilities. The M4A1 has a rifling twist of one in seven inches making it compatible with the full range of 5.56mm ammunitions. Its sighting system contains dual apertures, allowing for zero to two hundred meters and a smaller opening for engaging targets at a longer range of five hundred to six hundred meters.

Special Operations Peculiar Modification (SOPMOD) Accessory Kit

U.S. Special Operations forces wanted to make the M4A1 carbine even more effective, whether close-in engagements or long-range targets. To accomplish this USSOCOM and Crane Division, Naval Surface Warfare Center, developed the

A combat controller operating in Afghanistan during Operation Enduring Freedom. He wears a Blackhawk strike vest with an assortment of pouches and pockets. He is armed with an M4A1 with an Aimpoint Comp-M sight. The sight superimposes a red dot on the target, which the brain sees, allowing the soldier to adjust his weapon accordingly when required in the fast-paced shooting environment of CBQ. The Comp-M is parallax free, which means the shooter does not have to compensate for parallax deviation. *U.S. Air Force*

Special Operations peculiar modification (SOPMOD) accessory kit. Introduced in 1994, the SOPMOD kit is issued to all U.S. Special Operations forces to expand on the capabilities and operation of the M4A1 carbine.

The SOPMOD kit consists of numerous components that may be attached directly on the M4A1 carbine or attached to the rail interface system (RIS). The various accessories give the operator the flexibility to choose the appropriate, optics, lasers, lights, etc., dependent on mission parameters. The SOPMOD kit is constantly being evaluated and research is ongoing to further enhance the operability, functionality, and lethality of the M4A1 carbine. Currently, the kit is in Block 1 of a three-phase upgrade and modification program. STS battlefield airmen will also utilize other military and commercially off the shelf (COTS) modifications to enhance the M4A1 and the SOPMOD kit dependent on mission parameters, as seen in the embedded additions to the accessories below.

Rail Interface System (RIS)

The rail interface system (RIS) is a notched rail system, which replaces the front hand guards on the M4A1 receiver. This rail system is located on the top, bottom, and sides of the barrel, and facilitates the attaching of SOPMOD kit components on any of the four sides. The notches are numbered making it possible to attach, and re-attached the various components at the same position each time it is mounted. Optical sights and night-vision devices can be mounted on the top, while top and side rails would be the choice for positioning laser-aiming devices or lights. The bottom of the RIS normally will accommodate the vertical grip and/or lights. When no accessories are mounted to the RIS, plastic hand guards are emplaced to provide cover and protect the unused portions of the rail.

ACOG (Advance Combat Optical Gunsight)

The ACOG manufactured by Trijicon is the day optical scope for the SOPMOD kit. The ACOG is a four power telescopic sight including a ballistic compensating reticle. Utilizing this reticle provides increased capability to direct, identify, and hit target to the maximum effective range of the M4A1 carbine (six hundred meters). As a backup, the ACOG is equipped

The EOTech SU-231/PEQ holographic display sight (HDS) uses the same technology as is found in the heads up display, or HUD, on the F-117 aircraft. As the name implies, it displays holographic patterns, which have been designed for instant target acquisition under any lighting situations, without covering or obscuring the point of aim. The holographic reticle can be seen through the sight providing the operator with a large view of the target or zone of engagement. Using both eyes open the operator sights in on the target for a true two-eye operation.

The heads up, rectangular, full view of the SU-231/PEQ HDS eliminates any blind spots, constricted vision, or tunnel vision normally associated with cylindrical lights. The HDS is passive and gives off no signature, which could be seen by using units using NVGs. Having ten NV settings, the reticle will not "bloom" when viewed through night vision equipment. When used in conjunction with the AN/PVS-14 night vision device, it provides the operator with an outstanding view of the target area, and immediate target acquisition even in the darkest of environments.

with an iron sight for rapid close range engagement (CRE). Both the front iron sight and the scope reticle provide target recognition and stand-off attack advantage while retaining a close quarter capability equivalent to the standard iron sights.

Aimpoint Comp-M

After extensive testing, the U.S. Army adopted the Aimpoint Comp-M as its red dot sighting system. Using a both eyes open and heads up method, the shooter is able to acquire the target with excellent speed and accuracy. The Comp-M sight superimposes a red dot on the target, which the brain sees, allowing the soldier to adjust his weapon accordingly when required in the fast-pace shooting environment of CBQ. The Comp-M is parallax free, which means the shooter does not have to compensate for parallax deviation. The sight may be mounted on the carrying handle or RIS of the M4A1.

SU-231/PEQ

The SU-231/PEQ is part of the subprogram of the SOP-MOD kit. Manufactured by EOTech, the holographic display sight, as the name implies, displays holographic patterns, which have been designed for instant target acquisition under any lighting situations, without covering or obscuring the point of aim. The holographic reticle can be seen through

The AN/PEQ-2 infrared target pointer/illuminator/aiming laser (ITPIAL) incorporates lessons learned from Desert Storm and other combat operations.

AN/PVS-14 is the optimum night-vision monocular for special applications. It can be used handheld, on a facemask, helmet mounted, or attached to the RIS/RAS of a weapon. The AN/PVS-14 manufactured by ITT offers the latest, state-of-the-art capability in a package that meets the rigorous demands of Special Operations forces. By using the monocular configuration, the user can operate with night vision, while maintaining night vision in the opposite eye.

the sight providing the operator with a large view of the target or zone of engagement. Unlike other optics, the SU-231/PEQ is passive and gives off no telltale signature. The heads up, rectangular, full view of the HDS eliminates any blind spots, constricted vision, or tunnel vision normally associated with cylindrical sights. Using both eyes open the operator sights in on the target for a true two-eye operation.

The wide field of view of the SU-231/PEQ allows the operator to sight in on the target/target area while maintaining peripheral viewing through the sight if needed, up to thirty five off axis. A unique feature of the HDS is the fact it works if the heads-up display window is obstructed by mud, snow, etc. Even if the laminated window is shattered, the sight remains fully operational, with the point of aim/impact being maintained. Since many of special tactics teams' missions favor the night, it can be used in conjunction with NVG/NVD. The hallmarks of the HDS are speed and ease of use equating incredible accuracy and instant sight on target operation, which can be the difference between life and death in CQB operations.

Night Vision
AN/PVS-14

The AN/PVS-14D is the optimum night-vision monocular ensemble for special applications. The monocular or pocket-scope can be handheld, on a facemask, helmet mounted, or attached to a weapon. The new PVS-14D night-vision monocular offers the latest, state-of-the-art capability in a package that meets the rigorous demands of the U.S. military's Special Operations forces. The monocular configuration is important to shooters who want to operate with night vision, while maintaining dark adaptation in the opposite eye. The headmount assembly, a standard in the kit, facilitates hands-free operation, when helmet wear is not required. The weapon mount allows for use in a variety of applications from

using your iron sights to coupling with a red dot or tritium sighting system such as the Aimpoint Comp M/ML, Trijicon ACOG system, and EOTech HDS. A compass is available to allow the user to view the bearing in the night-vision image.

AN/PVS-17

The AN/PVS-17 is a lightweight, compact, night-vision sight that provides the operator the capability to locate, identify, and engage targets from twenty to three hundred meters. The MNVS features a wide field-of-view, magnified night-vision image, illuminated reticle, adjustable for windage/elevation. It can be handheld or mounted on the weapon.

AN/PEQ-2 infrared target pointer/ illuminator/ aiming laser (ITPIAL)

The AN/PEQ-2 infrared target pointer/illuminator/aiming laser (ITPIAL) allows the M4A1 to be effectively employed to three hundred meters with standard-issue night-vision goggles (NVGs) or a weapon-mounted night-vision device.

The quick attach/detach sound suppressor kit Mk4 MOD0 (QAD Suppressor) can quickly be emplaced or removed from the M4A1 carbine. With the suppressor in place, the report of the weapon is reduced by a minimum of 28 dB. The suppressor also reduces muzzle flash and blast substantially. This M4A1 is also equipped with the Surefire Millennium M900A vertical foregrip weapon light. *U.S. Air Force*

The IR illuminator broadens the capabilities of the NVGs in buildings, tunnels, jungle, overcast, and other low-light conditions, where starlight would not be sufficient to support night vision and allows visibility in areas normally in shadow. At close range, a neutral density filter is used to eliminate flare around the aiming laser for improving the view of the target, for identification, as well as precision aiming. This combination provides the operator a decisive advantage over an opposing force with little or no night-vision capability.

Forward Handgrip

The forward or vertical handgrip attaches to the bottom of the RIS and provides added support giving the operator a more stable firing platform. It can be used as a monopod in a supported position and allows the operator to hold the weapon despite overheating. The forward handgrip can be used to push against the assault sling and stabilize the weapon with isometric tension during CQB/CRE. Using the handgrip

The M203 grenade launcher is a lightweight, single-shot breech-loaded 40mm weapon specifically designed for placement beneath the barrel of the M4A1 carbine. With a quick-release mechanism, the addition of the M203 to M4A1 carbine creates the versatility of a weapon system capable of firing both 5.56mm ammunition as well as an expansive range of 40mm high-explosive and special-purpose munitions. *U.S. Air Force*

brings the shooter's elbows in closer or tighter to his body consequently keeping the weapon in front of the operator. The handle allows quicker handling when the additional components have been attached to the weapon, thus providing more precise target acquisition.

Having numerous modifications available it tends to make the solider want to use them all; it is not uncommon to see an operator with as many of the SOPMOD accessories on the M4A1 as he can fit. One operator commented on the use of the vertical grip, "One of the drawbacks of the vertical grip, often called the 'broom handle' is possibility of it catching on a ledge or edge of the helicopter during entry or extraction." This issue is being addressed by the evaluation of a quick release lever on the forward grip.

Crane Stock

A new modification to the M4A1 carbine is the addition of a redesigned collapsible stock. The stock was designed by the Crane Division of the Naval Surface Warfare Center (NSWC), Crane, Indiana, and is referred to as the M14 stock, or simply the crane stock. The new stock affords the operator with a larger surface giving him a better position for placing his cheek. This "spot weld" provides the user with a more comfortable and stabile firing position than the current tubular design. The wider stock also features storage on both sides, which will accommodate extra batteries for such items as NVGs, flashlights, GPS, etc.

Quick Attach Suppressor

The quick attach/detach sound suppressor kit Mk4 MOD0 (QAD suppressor) can quickly be emplaced or removed from the M4A1 carbine. With the suppressor in place, the report of the weapon is reduced by a minimum of 28 decibels (dB). As the 5.56mm round is supersonic, you will hear an audible crack of the round as it exits the barrel, but it is more like a .22 caliber pistol than a 5.56mm round. With the suppressor attached, it buys some time, while the bad guys are trying to figure out what was that? Where did it come from? By the time they figure out what is going on, the assault team should be in control of the situation. The suppressor will also keep the muzzle blast to a minimum, assisting the entry team in

The SCAR-H will replace the MK11 and the M14/enhanced battle rifle. Both SCAR models feature three interchangeable variable length barrels: CQC, standard, and sniper variant. This allows the special tactics squadron team member to fine-tune his weapon base on mission parameters. *FNH USA Photo*

situation awareness. While the suppressor does not completely eliminate the sound, it does reduce the firing signature (i.e., the flash and muzzle blasts). Using the suppressor is effective as a deceptive measure interfering with the enemy's ability to locate the shooter and take immediate action. Additionally, it reduces the need for hearing protection during CQB/CRE engagements thus improving inter-team voice communication.

Back-up Iron Sight (BUIS)

The back-up iron sight (BUIS) supplies aiming ability similar to the standard iron sight on the carbine to three hundred meters. The BUIS folds out of the way to allow the day optical scope or reflex sight and night-vision device to be mounted on the M4A1 carbine. In the event the optical scopes are damaged or otherwise rendered inoperable, they can be removed and the BIS will then be used to complete the mission. The sight can also be used to bore sight or confirm zero on the reflex sight or visible laser.

M203 Grenade Launcher

The quick attach/detach M203 mount and leaf sight when combined with the standard M203 grenade launcher provides additional firepower to the operator giving him both a point and area engagement capability. The most commonly utilized ammunition is the M406 40mm projectile, which includes high-explosive, dual-purpose ammunition; this grenade has a deadly radius of five meters, and it used as anti-personnel and anti-light armor. The quick-attach M203 combines flexibility and lethality to the individual weapon, utilizing multiple M203 setups, allowing concentrated fire by bursting munitions. These munitions are extremely useful in raids and ambushes or the ability to illuminate or obscure the target along with simultaneously delivering continuous HEDP fire. The M203 grenade leaf sight attaches to the rail interface system for fire control.

The receiver of the M203 is manufactured of high strength forged aluminum alloy. This provides extreme

When the mission calls for quietly reaching out and touching someone, the MK 11 has the ability to mount a sound suppresser. The muzzle blast becomes negligible and the only sound here is the sonic crack of the round going down range. The Mark 11 Mod 0 Type Rifle System 7.62mm is manufactured by Knight Manufacturing Company in Florida, it is a highly accurate, precision semi-automatic sniper rifle chamber capable of delivering its 7.62mm round well out to one thousand yards. This MK11 Mod 0 is equipped with a Leupold Long Range Tactical 3.5-10X 40mm Scope. *Knight Manufacturing Company*

ruggedness, while keeping weight to a minimum. A complete self-cocking firing mechanism, including striker, trigger, and positive safety lever, is included in the receiver. This will allow the M203 to be operated as an independent weapon, even though attached to the M16A1, M16A2 rifles, and M4A1 carbine. The barrel is also made of high strength aluminum alloy, which has been shortened from twelve to nine inches, allowing improved balance and handling. It slides forward in the receiver to accept a round of ammunition then slides backward to automatically lock in the closed position, ready to fire.

Carrying out their missions in small teams, special tactics teams depend on rapid deployment, mobility, and increased firepower; where the emphasis is focused on "get in and get out" fast, the addition of the M203 brings the added firepower to the M4A1 carbine.

Special Operations Forces Combat Assault Rifle (SCAR)

Currently, the special tactics teams are using the M4A1 carbine; however, plans are in place to fully update the teams to the Special Operations forces combat assault rifle (SCAR), to be fielded by 2009. The SCAR is a modular assault rifle designed from the ground up with input from U.S. Special Operations forces. Designed by FN Herstal (FNH) Group headquartered in Liege, Belgium; the SCAR will be manufactured at the FN Manufacturing LLC plant in Columbia, South Carolina.

The SCAR system includes the SCAR-L (light) 5.56mm, SCAR-H (heavy) 7.62mm rifle, version and enhanced grenade launcher module (EGLM), which will be able to fire air burst munitions, as well as standard 40mm, high-explosive, dual-purpose ammunition. There is a ninety percent commonality between the two SCAR versions. The SCAR-L and SCAR-H utilize all of the accessories of the SOPMOD kit; (i.e., sights, lasers, scopes, etc.). To accommodate the assortment of SOPMOD accessories, the SCAR has multiple Picatiny (MIL-STD 1913) rails at 3-6-9-12 o'clock positions providing the operators with multiple configurations.

The SCAR-L will replace the MK18 CQBR (ten-inch SOPMOD upper), standard M4A1 carbine, and the MK12 SPR. The SCAR-H will replace the MK11 and the M14/enhanced battle rifle. Both SCAR models feature three interchangeable variable length barrels; for CQC, standard and sniper variant. This allows the special tactics squadron team member to fine-tune his weapon base on mission parameters.

The SCAR weapons employ a short stroke gas piston system eliminating the gas direct system of the M16/M4 family. This provides a more reliable weapon that does not heat up the rail system. The butt-stock features a folding telescoping stock as well as check height adjustment. This allows the operator to set the proper eye alignment to the assortment of SOPMOD optics.

To complement the SCAR is the enhanced grenade launcher module (EGLM), which replaces the M203 grenade launcher. The 40mm EGLM features a left- or right-hand side opening breech to facilitate the loading of longer munitions. The EGLM includes a 40mm weapon module, Fired Control Unit I (mechanical with integrated laser/MRD sight) and a standalone stock.

MK11

The MK11 Mod 0 type rifle system 7.62mm, manufactured by Knight Manufacturing Company in Florida, is a highly accurate, precision semi-automatic sniper rifle chamber capable of delivering its 7.62mm round well out to one thousand yards. With a half-inch MOA accuracy, the MK11 has won acceptance in the SOF community as one of the finest semi-automatic sniper rifles in the world. The MK11 is based on the original SR-25; this rifle appears to be an M16 on steroids. In fact sixty percent of the parts are common with the M16 family.

M249 Squad Assault Weapon is an individually portable, air-cooled, belt-fed, gas-operated, light machinegun. The standard ammunition load is two hundred rounds of 5.56mm ammunition in disintegrating belts. These rounds are fed from a two hundred–round plastic ammunition box and fed through the side of the weapon. Utilizing the same 5.56mm ammunition as the M4A1, it allows the ODA to carry common ammunition loads. The M249 is capable of engaging targets out to eight hundred meters. The STS teams will soon be fielding the MK46, which is a modified version of the SAW. *U.S. Air Force*

The M240B is the replacement for the aging M60 machinegun. The highly reliable 7.62mm machine gun delivers more energy to the target than the smaller caliber M249 squad assault weapon (SAW). The machinegun seen here is a M240B mounted on a M1114 ground mobility vehicle. To augment battlefield airmen's range and lethality, they will be adding the MK48 to their inventory, which is a modified version of the M240 weapon. *U.S. Air Force*

If an operator is familiar with the M16 or M4A1, his hands will naturally fall in place on the MK11. From the pistol grip, to the safety switch or magazine release, if you've handled an M16 you already know how to operate the MK11. The result of this replication is a rifle that is quicker to assimilate, easy to maintain, and seamless in transition than any other semi-automatic 7.62mm rifle in the world.

Similar to the M4A1, the MK11 has two main sections; the upper and lower receiver. This allows for cleaning in the same manner that the troops have been familiar with since basic training. Another benefit of the receiver's breakdown is the fact that the rifle may be transported in a smaller package for clandestine activities. Once on target, the rifle is merely reassembled with no effect on the zero of the optics.

The MK11 Mod 0 system includes free floating twenty-inch barrel, and a free-floating rail adapter system (RAS). The RAS is similar to the RIS on the M4A1. Another feature of the MK11 is the ability to mount a sound suppresser. The muzzle blast becomes negligible and the only sound here is the sonic crack of the round going down range.

M249 Squad Automatic Weapon (SAW)

Fielded in the mid-eighties, the M249 SAW is an individually portable, air-cooled, belt-fed, gas-operated, light machinegun. A unique feature of the SAW is the number of alternate ammunition feeds. The standard ammunition load is two hundred rounds of 5.56mm ammunition in disintegrating belts. These rounds are fed from a two hundred–round plastic ammunition box and feed through the side of the weapon. The normal link ammunition for the SAW is four rounds of M855 ball ammunitions followed by one round of M85 tracer. Additionally, it can utilize standard twenty- and thirty-round M16 magazines, which are inserted in a magazine well in the bottom of the SAW. Utilizing the same 5.56mm ammunition as the M4A1, it allows the ODA to carry common ammunition loads. The M249 is capable of engaging targets out to eight hundred meters. Currently, the M249 in use with special tactics teams is fitted with a full stock and not with a sliding stock as used in the para-saw configuration.

The STS teams will soon be fielding the MK 46 MOD 0 light machine gun, which is a modified version of the M249 Saw. The MK46 is upgraded with the rail attachment system, allowing the attachment of SOPMOD kit accessories. The MK46 is an air-cooled, belt-fed, gas-operated automatic weapon that fires from the open-bolt position. It has a cyclic rate of 750 rounds per minute and can be fitted with a standard thirty-round M4A1 magazine or a 200-round box magazine.

M240B Medium Machine Gun

After extensive operational testing, the M240 medium machine gun was selected as a replacement for the M60 family of machine guns. Manufactured by Fabrique Nationale the 24.2-pound M240 medium machinegun is a gas-operated, air-cooled, linked belt-fed weapon that fires the 7.62x51mm

The Mark 47 advanced lightweight grenade launcher is a self-powered, air-cooled, belt-fed, blow-back operated weapon. The MK47 is designed to deliver accurate, intense, and decisive firepower against enemy personnel and lightly armored vehicle. It uses standard belt-fed 40mm ammunition in either M430 high-explosive, dual-purpose (HEDP) or the MK285 air bursting ammunition. *U.S. Air Force*

round. The weapon fires from an open bolt position with a maximum effective range of eleven hundred meters. The rate of fire is adjustable from seven hundred fifty to one thousand, four hundred rounds per minute through an adjustable gas regulator. It features a folding bipod that attaches to the receiver, a quick-change barrel assembly, a feed cover and bolt assembly enabling closure of the cover regardless of bolt position, a plastic butt stock, and an integral optical sight rail. While it possessed many of the same characteristics as the older M60, the durability of the M240 system results in superior reliability and maintainability.

The special tactics teams are transitioning to the customized MK48 Light machinegun that allows for the attachment of SOP mod accessories (e.g., optical sights, night-vision devices, laser designators, IR aiming devices, flashlights, and a forward pistol grip or bi-pod).

AT4

The M136 AT4 is the U.S. Army's principal light anti-tank weapon providing precision delivery of an 84mm, high-explosive, anti-armor warhead, with negligible recoil. The M136 AT4 is a man-portable, self-contained, anti-armor weapon consisting of a free-flight, fin-stabilized, rocket-type cartridge packed in an expendable, one-piece, fiberglass-wrapped tube. Unlike the M72 LAAW, the AT4 launcher does not need to

be extended before firing. When the warhead makes impact with the target, the nosecone crushes and the impact sensor activates the internal fuse.

Upon ignition, the piezoelectric fuse element triggers the detonator, initiating the main charge. This results in penetration where the main charge fires and sends the warhead body into a directional gas jet, which is capable of penetrating over seventeen inches of armor plate. The after effects are "spalling"; the projecting of fragments and incendiary effects generate blinding light and obliterate the interior of the target.

Load Bearing Equipment (LBE)

It began with stuffing extra magazines into BDU pockets, then pouches and vests. Today, dependant on the mission, the most common way of carrying gear is in an assault vest or chest harness. Attached to the pistol belts, assault vests provide an easy access to ammunition and other items during the fast-paced CQB mission. On the front of the vest, pouches may hold magazines for M4A1 5.56mm, MP5 9mm, or 7.62mm depending on the weapon of choice for the operator. Small pockets and pouches are readily available to accommodate pistol magazines, shotgun shells, first aid field dressing, flex cuffs, strobes, chem-lights, pressure dressings, or grenades (e.g., smoke, stun, CS gas, and fragmentation). Some vest designs are of a modular nature, where the vest is made up of attachment points via Velcro, Alice clips, or other fasteners. These systems allow for the modification of the user's vest with assorted holsters, magazine pouches, radio pockets, etc. Internal pockets allow the operators to stow maps or other gear. Additionally, these vests may have various-sized back pouches to accommodate such items as gas masks, helmets, demolition equipment, and other mission-essential items.

Recently, as seen in Operations Enduring Freedom and Iraqi Freedom, many of the SOF operators are gravitating to the chest harness. A number of manufacturers feature such COTS harnesses (e.g., Blackhawk Industries, High Speed Gear, Eagle, and Tactical Tailor). While assault vests and LBE continues to be used by the teams, a number of the special tactics team members are migrating to the chest harness. The larger pouches will accommodate two to three M4, 30-round magazines depending on the manufacturer. The other pouches will accommodate such items as hydration systems, radios, MRE, compass, laser pointer, or other mission-essential equipment.

The team's SOP will determine the layout of the mission-essential gear. All team members are sure of each member's equipment capabilities, equipment is exchangeable, training continuity is achievable, and less variation in team equipment means fewer problems to consider. Another requisite item worn on the vests is the U.S. flag, most often an IR version.

GPS

Whether its AFSOC Pave Low pilots navigating to exact locations through the mountains, or STS teams conducting reconnaissance and surveillance over sand dunes and wadis in the dead of night, teams rely on global positioning systems to perform these tasks.

The precise name for the Rockwell "Plugger," or PSN-11, is PLGR96 (precise lightweight GPS receiver). The PLGR96 is the most advanced version of the U.S. Department of Defense handheld GPS units. It addresses the increasingly demanding requirements of the U.S. Special Operations forces.

Secure (Y-code) differential GPS (SDGPS) allows the user to accept differential correction without zeroing the unit. Other features of the Plugger include wide-area GPD enhancement (WAGE) for autonomous positioning accuracy to four meters CEP, jammer direction finding, targeting interface with

A pair of M136 AT4 light anti-tank weapons can be seen in the back seat of this NSTV. The AT4 provides precision delivery of an 84mm high-explosive, anti-armor warhead, with negligible recoil. The AT4 is a man-portable, self-contained, anti-armor weapon consisting of a free-flight, fin-stabilized, rocket-type cartridge packed in an expendable, one-piece, fiberglass-wrapped tube. The warhead is capable of penetrating more than seventeen inches of armor plate, the aftereffects are "spalling" the projecting of fragments and incendiary effects generating blinding light and obliterating the interior of the target. Note the M60 7.62mm machinegun equipped with ACOG and AN/PEQ-2. *U.S. Air Force*

laser range-finder, remote display terminal capability, and advanced user interface features.

Weighing in at a mere 2.7 pounds (with batteries installed), the GPS unit is easily stowed in the cavernous rucksack that the STS troops carry. In addition to handheld operation, the PLGR96 unit can be installed into various vehicles and airborne platforms.

While all special tactics teams are schooled in land navigation using the standard issue Lensetic compass, it is equally important for the teams to be able to have pinpoint accuracy when conducting a DA mission through the desert, or across the frozen tundra, in enemy territory, in the middle of the night. They will need to know the position of a terrorist's hideout, a radar station, or perhaps a WMD cache when reporting into headquarters. For such instances they will utilize a device known as a global positioning system.

The GPS is a collection of satellites that orbit the earth twice a day. During this orbiting, they transmit the precise

Working together with the Special Forces, battlefield airmen hitch a ride with the 3rd SFG. The ground mobility vehicle (GMV) had its origins in Desert Storm. During the Gulf War, the Special Forces–modified HUMMVs were used for extended desert missions and dubbed as the DUMMVs, pronounced—"Dum-Vees." The modifications included a heavier suspension, more powerful engine, an open bed, and back for storage of water and fuel and other mission essential items. This GMV is armed with an M2 .50-caliber machinegun and an M240B 7.62mm machine gun. *U.S. Air Force*

A member of the STT races down the tarmac still carrying his rucksack and armed with an M4. He will search the runway for foreign object damage (FOD). Anything that may hamper the follow-on forces from landing will be dealt with expeditiously. If necessary, CCTs are trained to remove such obstacles with explosives.

A special tactics squadron team member takes a break as he poses with one of the team's non-standard tactical vehicles (NSTV). These Toyota pickup trucks are everywhere in Afghanistan allowing the SOF teams to infiltrate with more ease in their hunt for Taliban and al-Qaeda forces. He is armed with an M4A1 assault rifle, though he has traded the standard BDUs for more covert attire. *U.S. Air Force*

This Polaris all-terrain vehicle (ATV) has a variety of uses for the STT. It is air droppable expediting an airfield survey and may be set up with an assortment of radio equipment to facilitate the ATC mission of the CCTs. It can be set up to shuttle supplies or wounded from point-to-point for the PJs. Using the quad, the STT can quickly maneuver from one area of the airhead to another as the mission unfolds. These STS team members have stopped to take some wind measurements. *U.S. Air Force*

The ATVs are in use by STT conducting search and destroy missions as they hunt down Taliban and al-Qaeda forces. This Polaris ATV is loaded down with mission-essential gear as special tactics teams carry out their missions in the cold wasteland of Afghanistan in support of Operation Enduring Freedom. This combat controller is armed with an M4A1 carbine and is wearing AN/AVS-6V3 NVGs to maneuver through the moonless night. *U.S. Air Force*

Having parachuted into an airfield prior to the follow-on forces, this combat controller prepares to activate the TACAN mounted on the rear of a quad. The TACAN is an omni-directional navigation beacon, which will be used by the incoming aircraft.

Whether speeding down the tarmac of a captured airfield or busting through the bush, the rescue all terrain transport (RATT) is well designed to meet the demanding needs of the AFSOC STS troopers' RATT. Designed to AFSOC specifications, this vehicle is used by special tactics squadrons. It can be fitted with litters to accommodate the pararescue men doing combat triage.

time, latitude, longitude, and altitude information. Using a GPS receiver, Special Operations forces can ascertain their exact location anywhere on the earth.

AN/PEQ-1A SOFLAM

When it absolutely, positively has to be destroyed, you put an SOF team on the ground and a fast mover with a smart bomb in the air and the result is one smoking bomb crater. The Special Operations forces laser acquisition marker (SOFLAM) is lighter and smaller than the current laser marker in service with the U.S. military. It provides the STT with the capability to locate and designate critical enemy targets for destruction using laser-guided ordnance. It can be used in daylight or with the attached night-vision optics, it can be employed at night.

Northrop Grumman's ground laser target designator (GLTD II), a.k.a. the SOFLAM, is a compact, lightweight, portable laser target designator and rangefinder. The SOFLAM is capable of exporting range data via an RS422

An STS combat controller places an IR signaling light in preparation for a helicopter insertion. Special tactics squadrons are a combination of combat controllers, pararescuemen, and occasionally Special Operations weather teams. These highly trained battlefield airmen are experts in ATC, CAS, emergency trauma medicine, and forecasting.

link and importing azimuth and elevation. It was designed to enable Special Operations forces to direct laser-guided smart weapons, such as Paveway bombs, Hellfire missiles, and Copperhead munitions. The AN/PEQ-1A can be implemented as part of a sophisticated, digitized fire-control system with thermal or image-intensified sights.

The SOFLAM uses the PRF or pulse repetition frequency that can be set to NATO STANAG Band I or II or is programmable. (Note: STANAG represents standards and agreements set forth by NATO for the process, procedures, terms, and conditions under which Mutual Government Quality Assurance of defense products are to be performed by the APPROPRIATE NATIONAL AUTHORITY of one NATO member nation, at the request of another NATO member nation or NATO Organization.) PRF is the number of pulses per second transmitted by a laser.

Radios

One of the most awesome weapons in the inventory of the special tactics squadron is without a doubt their radio. A veteran combat controller relates, "When the lead starts flying, the shooters think in terms of 'head to ground,' the STS team thinks in terms of 'head and above.'" During OEF, for every one kill a combat controller made with his M4A1 carbine, he made 168 with CAS called in on his radio.

Communication is paramount in the arsenal of the STS team. You see it when they take off their floppy hats and the head gear of the interteam radio is visible. It is there when the team unfolds the umbrella-like satellite antennae and connects it to the compact PRC-117F. Whether using UHF, VHF, line of sight, or SATCOM, the STS teams maintain the vital link between their unit and the air assets. With this, they can call in the full weight of an AC-130U gunship circling overhead or an MH-53E Pave Low, orbiting just beyond the ridge line. As Senior Master Sgt. Philip Rhodes, AFSOC PAO reports, "... (An) STS team on the ground and a gunship in the air is a lethal combination."

Land navigation is an essential skill for all Special Operations operators. Knowing the location of the insertion LZ, the coordinates for the smart bomb is not insignificant, where is the extraction point. Special tactics teams get training in land navigation to facilitate their mission success. The Rockwell precision lightweight GPS receiver, or PLGR96 referred to as the "Plugger," will continuously track up to five satellites. The unit is sealed for operations in all environments, and computes accurately position coordinates, elevation, speed, and time data from transmitted signals from orbiting GPS satellites.

AN/PRC-117F

Communications is the lifeline of any special tactics team on a mission. For long-range communications, the AN/PRC-117F covers the entire 30 to 512 MHz frequency range while offering embedded COMSEC, and Havequick I/II ECCM capabilities. This advanced software reprogrammable digital radio supports continuous operation across the 90 to 420 MHz band providing 20 W FM and 10 W AM transmit power with Havequick I/II capability (10 W FM in other frequency ranges).

It can be used in conjunction with the KY-57/TSEC speech security equipment for secure voice communications. The radio supports both DS-101 and DS-102 fill interfaces and all common fill devices for Havequick Word-of-Day (WOD) and encryption key information. This device supports the Department of Defense requirement for a lightweight, secure, network-capable, multi-band,

When it absolutely, positively has to be destroyed, you put a SOF team on the ground and a fast mover with a smart bomb in the air. The PEQ-1A SOFLAM, weighing twelve pounds, is a man-portable laser designator used to mark targets for laser-guided ordnance and a laser range finder for determining the distance to a target.

Pictured is the business end of an AN/PEQ-1A laser designator. The SOFLAM uses the pulse repetition frequency (PRF) that can be set to NATO STANAG Band I or II or is programmable. The PRF is the number of pulses per second transmitted by a laser. Before the pilot releases his ordinance, the aircraft's computer indicates to the bomb's control system a specific pattern, the PRF. Once the smart bomb is released, it will home in on that specific pulse pattern; guiding in on the SOFLAM signal, the ordnance will find its way directly to the target. This is often referred to as "painting the target."

multi-mission, anti-jam, voice/imagery/data communication capability in a single package.

PRC/148 MBITR

Thales Communication multiband inter/intrateam radio (MBITR) is a powerful tactical handheld radio designed for the U.S. Special Operations Command. The MBITR more than met the tough SOCOM requirements and provides a secure voice and digital-data radio with exceptional versatility, ruggedness, and reliability.

The immersable unit weighs less than two pounds and includes a keypad, graphics display, and built-in speaker-microphone. Typical of the advanced designs of Thales radios, MBITR utilizes digital-signal processing and flash memory to support functions traditionally performed by discrete hardware in other manufacturers' equipment. The power output is up to five watts over the 30- to 512-MHz frequency band. The MBITR has embedded Type 1 COMSEC for both voice and data traffic.

Battlefield Air Operations Kit

Depending on the mission being conducted by the special tactics team, these airmen will carry a wide variety of equipment, which may include: UHF/VHF radio, intrateam radio, headsets, GPS units, SOFLAM, Laser Ranger finder, Laser pointers, scopes, thermal video, beacons, tactical UAV, Panasonic "Toughbook" computer, extra batteries, food, water, ammunition along with primary and secondary weapons. When you add it up, the total weight of the equipment will often exceed that of the operator.

This fact was not lost on AFSOC and they went to work evaluating equipment, military as well as COTS, which was lighter, smaller, and was multi-functional with an ease of deployment. Today, what used to weigh in at more than one hundred pounds now weighs approximately seventy-five pounds. The improved equipment is lighter weight and more compact. Known as the battlefield air operations (BAO) kit, it allows the combat controller to insert more efficiently and effectively behind enemy lines.

The BAO kit contains laser designators, scopes thermal imagers, and range finders. All this data along with the GPS coordinates are fed into the combat controller's computer. From there specially designed software allows the controller to transmit targeting data to the command and control element who will make the decision to destroy the target or pass the information on to other aircraft.

A feature of the BAO kit allows the combat controller to send intelligence directly from machine-to-machine, called M2M instead of human to human, to avoid targeting errors. The Net-centric methodology allows the combat controller to use what is known as cursor-on-target. The concept is to place the data from system to system while the human element controls the military decision.

The BAO kit is constantly evolving as new technology and equipment becomes available. Just as the combination of the cell phone, camera, and Internet in a handheld PDA, which is commonplace in any office, AFSOC endeavors to combine various equipment into compact devices to serve the special tactics team members in the field. While technology is a wonderful thing, it must be remembered that to be of any tactical value it must be placed in the hand of the battlefield airman.

Above: Thales' multiband inter/intrateam radio (MBITR) is a powerful tactical handheld radio designed for the U.S. Special Operations Command. Designated the AN/PRC148, it provides a secure voice and digital-data radio with exceptional versatility, ruggedness, and reliability. The immersible unit weighs less than two pounds and includes a keypad, graphics display, and built-in speaker-microphone. The MBITR has embedded Type 1 COMSEC for both voice and data traffic. *U.S. Air Force*

Left: "Call for Fire." An STS team leader calls in coordinates to the AC-130U Spooky gunship on station using an AN/PRC-117, while his teammate provides cover with a GUU-5/P. A special tactics team on the ground and a gunship overhead is a lethal combination.

Chapter 9

FUTURE OF AFSOC

The twenty-first century AFSOC warrior will be able to communicate better and evaluate intelligence faster than any of his predecessors. The battlefield airman of AFSOC will be equipped with the latest technology. As part of the SOF Warfighter Information Process Enhancements (SWIPE) Initiative during the Joint Expeditionary Force Experiment (JEFX) the STT will employ new information technology, Panasonic's Toughbook computer. Using this computer, the team can encompass a target from various positions. The wireless computers serve as a network where each team member can send information to the team leader, or "hub." The gathered intelligence, digital photos, or video and reports can then be shared with other teammates or sent via burst transmission over SATCOM to combatant commanders for review.

Unmanned aerial vehicles (UAVs) will continue to play a vital role as AFSOC prosecutes the Global War on Terrorism. The large Predator or the small hand-launched BatCam systems will help the aircrews above and the battlefield airmen on the ground to continue to excel at what they do best: raining down the might and power of the U.S. Air Force on the enemy.

As AFSOC continues to grow and evolve, the STS teams will see the infusion of high-tech equipment into their kit. The battlefield airmen of tomorrow will deploy with lighter, compact, and more capable equipment then ever before. This new technology with allow them to leverage an incredible amount of firepower on the enemy.

Today, combat controllers use an air traffic control simulator showing them views of numerous airports and airfields, viewed in a variety of weather conditions in night or daylight environments. When he hits the ground, he'll already be familiar with the lay of the land. Further research is being

Special tactics teams have been at the tip of the spear in the GWOT. The battlefield airman will provide operational depth to the theater combatant commander. Combat controllers as seen here are laden down with communications gear, GPS, computers, batteries, laser targeting equipment, sensors, food, batteries, and personal weapons. They are prepared to deal death upon the enemy or guide in aircraft carrying follow-on forces using their CAS or ATC skills, respectively, as required. The most lethal SOF operator on the ground is a STS team with a radio and a bomber, fast mover, or gunship overhead. *U.S. Air Force*

Left: An AFSOC CV-22 Osprey is silhouetted against the setting sun as it heads out for the evening's mission. The CV-22 will provide high speed time on target of an airplane, while operating as an insertion platform like a helicopter. The Osprey will conduct these missions with fewer incidents of aerial refueling thereby allowing covert SOF operations in one period of darkness. This aircraft will serve the Air Commandos providing agile clandestine mobility in placing Special Operations forces on target. *U.S. Air Force*

Above: "When in Rome." A special tactics squadron combat controller wears the local garb as he operates with SOF units in Afghanistan during Operation Enduring Freedom. Dressed in such manner allows the special operations warriors to blend into their surroundings. As long as these men are operating 'down range', no enemy is safe. They are the point of the eagle's talons as they hunt down high-value targets to bring them to justice, or bring justice to them. *U.S. Air Force*

AFSOC airman with computer JEFX: The twenty-first-century AFSOC warrior will be able to communicate better and evaluate intelligence faster than any of his predecessors. Here, an airman uses a Panasonic "Toughbook" computer, which is part of the SOF Warfighter Information Process Enhancements (SWIPE) Initiative during the Joint Expeditionary Force Experiment (JEFX). This airman is evaluating information processing enhancements, which enable him to gather intelligence, digital photos, or video and write up reports, which can then be shared with other teammates or sent via burst transmission over SATCOM to combatant commanders for further review. *U.S. Air Force*

Scout/Swimmer of a STT breaks the surface of the water and prepares to "recon" the beachhead. Once all is clear, he will signal the rest of the team to come ashore and they will begin their stealthy movement to their objective. With all the high-tech weaponry and equipment, it is still the warrior on the ground that brings all this gear to life.

done with special helmets that are linked to computers and satellites. These units will provide the wearer with tactical information via a heads-up display or HUD unit in the visor. Combat controllers will be able to see navigational data on the visor, while the PJ may bring up a procedure from a medical library contained in a computer in their rucksack. Holographic devices, improved night-vision goggles (NVGs), and thermal imagers may be found in the rucksacks of the STT in the not-so-distant future.

Today, the world is at war against fanatical Islam fascism. Just as they did more than sixty years ago, the Air Commandos of today stand poised to combat the threat to liberty and freedom. Faced with some of the most austere

conditions in the world, against an enemy that has no soul, AFSOC personnel are ready to carry out their missions.

The crew of an MC-130H will penetrate enemy air defenses to deliver an SOF team. A Combat Shadow will refuel a CV-22 somewhere over, oops—sorry, that's classified. Days before an assault, an STT will perform a regional survey of an HLZ; while a Pave Low will fly in under enemy radar, skimming above the terrain below, to perform a personnel recovery mission. An AC-130 gunship will be on station to provide CAS, and above them all will be a Predator providing intelligence and backup firepower if needed.

As America continues to wage the Global War on Terror, the men and women of AFSOC will remain at the tip of the

As AFSOC enters the next millennium, special tactics squadrons will continue to be the tip of the spear in U.S. Special Operations forces. They will more often than not be onsite before any other forces. They will often serve as the eyes and ears of USSOCOM, and if necessary they will bring in the muscle of the air assets of AFSOC, living up to their motto, "That others may live."

spear. When the President of the United States asks for "boots on the ground and eyes on the target," the first set of eyes will very likely be those of the Air Force Special Operations Command, special tactics teams. Whether it may be a combat controller, pararescueman, or Special Operations weathermen, these teams are masters of the art of war.

These are the Quiet Professionals of the U.S. Air Force Special Operations Command; the Air Commandos of the twenty-first century who carry on the tradition—ANYTIME, ANYPLACE.

Glossary

AT: Antiterrorism. Defensive measures used to reduce the vulnerability of individuals and property to terrorism.

Battlefield airmen: Air Force Special Operations Command special tactics squadron team members, combat controllers, pararescuemen, and Special Operations weather teams.

Battle rattle: Combat gear from body armor to load-bearing vest and all related equipment carried by the STT members.

C4I: Command, control, communications, computers, and intelligence.

CinC: Commander in chief. This refers exclusively to the President of the United States.

Civil affairs: The activities of a commander that establish, maintain, influence, or exploit relations between military forces and civil authorities, both governmental and non-governmental, and the civilian population in a friendly, neutral, or hostile area of operations to facilitate military operations and consolidate operational objectives. Civil affairs may include performance by military forces of activities and functions normally the responsibility of the local government. These activities may occur prior to, during, or subsequent to military action. They may also occur, if directed, in the absence of other military operations.

Clandestine operation: Activities sponsored or conducted by governmental departments or agencies in such a way as to ensure secrecy or concealment. (It differs from covert operations in that emphasis is placed on concealment of the operation rather than on concealment of the identity of the sponsor.) In Special Operations, an activity may be both covert and clandestine and may focus equally on operational considerations and intelligence-related activities.

Close air support (CAS): Air action against hostile targets that are in close proximity to friendly forces and require detailed integration of each air mission with the fire and movement of those forces.

Collateral special operations activities: Collateral activities in which Special Operations forces, by virtue of their inherent capabilities, selectively may be tasked to participate. These include security assistance, humanitarian assistance, antiterrorism and other security activities, counter-drug operations, personnel recovery, and special activities.

Counter-proliferation: Activities taken to counter the spread of dangerous military capabilities, and allied technologies or know-how, especially weapons of mass destruction and ballistic missile delivery systems.

Counter-terrorism: Offensive measures taken to prevent, deter, and respond to terrorism.

Covert operations: Operations planned and executed to conceal the identity of or permit plausible denial by the sponsor.

Direct action mission: In special operations, a specified act involving operations of an overt, covert, clandestine, or low-visibility nature conducted primarily by a sponsoring power's Special Operations forces in hostile or denied areas.

Ducks: Types of Zodiac deployments.

Double duck: Twin Zodiacs.

Hard: Zodiac with hard metal bottom.

K duck: Kangaroo.

Soft duck: Zodiac raft.

T duck: Tethered.

Exfiltration: The removal of personnel or units from areas under enemy control.

First-line belt: Specially designed webbing with a shock cord inside, used when traveling on aircraft. One end has a standard carabineer and the other end has a quick-release carabineer.

Foreign internal defense: Participation by civilian and military agencies of a government in any action programs taken by another government to free and protect its society from subversion, lawlessness, and insurgency.

Guerrilla warfare: Military and paramilitary operations conducted in enemy-held or hostile territory by irregular, predominantly indigenous forces.

Host nation: A nation that receives the forces or supplies of allied nations or NATO organizations to be located on, operated in, or transited through its territory.

Infiltration: The movement through or into an area or territory occupied by either friendly or enemy troops or organizations. The movement is made, either by small groups or by individuals, at extended or irregular intervals. When used in connection with the enemy, it implies that contact is avoided.

Insurgency: An organized movement aimed at the overthrow of a constituted government through the use of subversion and armed conflict.

Internal defense: The full range of measures taken by a government to free and protect its society from subversion, lawlessness, and insurgency.

Interoperability: The ability of systems, units, or forces to provide services to and to accept services from other systems, units, or forces, or use the services so exchanged to enable them to operate effectively together.

Low-intensity conflict: Political-military confrontation between contending states or groups below conventional war and above routine, peaceful competition among states. It frequently involves protracted struggles of competing principles and ideologies. Low-intensity conflict ranges from subversion to the use of armed force. It is waged by a combination of means employing political, economic, informational, and military instruments. Low-intensity conflicts are often localized, generally in the Third World, but contain regional and global security implications.

METT-T: Mission, Enemy, Troops, Terrain, and Time. Perimeters that affect the mission profile of the AFSOC task, including STS Personnel Recovery or AC-130 gunship CAS. These five criteria must be addressed in the mission planning.

Military civic action: The use of indigenous military forces on projects useful to the local population at all levels in such fields as education, training, public works, agriculture, transportation, communications, health, sanitation, and others contributing to economic and social development.

Mission: A statement of our reason for being and what we wish to accomplish as an organization.

NCA: National Command Authorities. The president and the secretary of defense together or their duly deputized alternates or successors. The term signifies constitutional authority to direct the Armed Forces in their execution of military action.

Objectives: Specific actions to be achieved in a specified time period. Accomplishment will indicate progress toward achieving the goals.

Ranger assist cord: A 550 cord (parachute line) used to attach anything and everything to an operator.

RAMZ: Rigging alternate method zodiac (pronounced "rams"). Procedure for air-dropping a Zodiac raft.

REDS: Rapid extrication deployment system, similar to the "jaws of life."

Special reconnaissance: Reconnaissance and surveillance actions conducted by Special Operations forces to obtain or verify, by visual observation or other collection methods, information concerning the capabilities, intentions, and activities of an actual or potential enemy or to secure data concerning the meteorological, hydrographic, or geographic characteristics of a particular area. It includes target acquisition, area assessment, and post-strike reconnaissance.

Strategy: Methods, approaches, or specific moves taken to implement and attain an objective.

Unconventional warfare: A broad spectrum of military and paramilitary operations conducted in enemy-held, enemy-controlled, or politically sensitive territory. Unconventional warfare includes, but is not limited to, the interrelated fields of guerrilla warfare, evasion and escape, subversion, sabotage, and other operations of a low-visibility, covert, or clandestine nature. These interrelated aspects of unconventional warfare may be prosecuted singularly or collectively by predominantly indigenous personnel, usually supported and directed in varying degrees by (an) external source(s) during all conditions of war or peace.

Acronyms and Abbreviations

AFSOC—Air Force Special Operations Command

AFSOF—Air Force Special Operations facility

ARSOC—U.S. Army Special Operations Command

CAP—Combat air patrol

CAS—Close air support

CCT—Combat control team

CIA—Central Intelligence Agency

CQB—Close quarters battle

CQBR—Close quarters battle receiver

CQC—Close quarters combat

CRO—Combat Rescue Officer

CRRC—Combat rubber raiding craft

CSAR—Combat search and rescue

CT—Counterterrorism

DA—Direct action

DOD—Department of Defense

DZ—Drop zone

E&E—Evasion and escape

EW—Electronic warfare

FAC—Forward air control

FID—Foreign internal defense

FLIR—Forward looking infrared

FOB—Forward operation base

FRIS—Fast rope insertion system

GPS—Global positioning system

GWOT—Global War On Terrorism

HAH—High altitude high opening

HALO—High altitude low opening

HE—High explosive

HEDP—High explosive dual purpose

HEI—High explosive incendiary

HUMINT—Human intelligence

IFAM—Initial familiarization

IIN—Integrated inertial navigation

INTREP—Intelligence report

JCS—Joint Chiefs of Staff

JTF—Joint Task Force

LBE—Load bearing equipment

LZ—Landing zone

MRE—Meal ready to eat

MTT—Mobile training team

NOE—Nape of the earth

NOD—Night optical device

NVG—Night-vision goggles

OEF—Operation Enduring Freedom

OGA—Other government agency—i.e., CIA

OIF—Operation Iraqi Freedom

PJ—Pararescue jumper

PR—Personnel recovery

PSYWAR—Psychological warfare

RAMZ—Rigid alternate method Zodiac

REDS—Rapid extrication deployment system

RST—Reconnaissance and surveillance team

SAR—Search and rescue

SAS—Special Air Service

SCAR—Special Operations forces combat assault rifle

SEAL—Sea Air Land (U.S. Navy Special Forces)

SF—Special Forces (U.S. Army)

SOCOM—Special Operations Command

SOF—Special Operations forces

SOFLAM—Special Operations forces laser acquisition marker

SOWT—Special Operations weather team

SPIES—Special procedure insertion extraction system

SR—Special reconnaissance

SST—SAR security team

STO—Special tactics officer

STS—Special tactics squadron

STT—Special tactics teams

USASOC—U.S. Army Special Operations Command

UW—Unconventional warfare

WMD—Weapons of mass destruction

Index

INDEX OF UNITS

INDEX OF WEAPONS

INDEX OF AIRCRAFT AND VEHICLES

GENERAL INDEX

Other **Zenith Press** titles of interest:

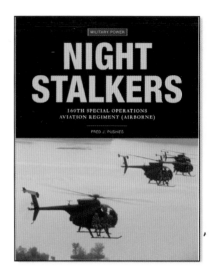

NIGHT STALKERS
978-07603-2141-6, 0-7603-2141-8

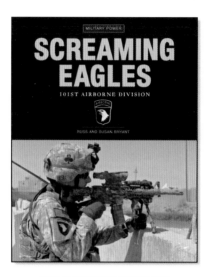

SCREAMING EAGLES
978-07603-3122-4, 0-7603-3122-7

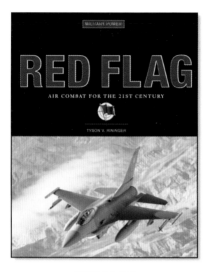

RED FLAG
978-0-7603-2530-8, 0-7603-2530-8

**WEAPONS OF
THE NAVY SEALS**
978-0-7603-1790-7, 0-7603-1790-9

FOUR STARS OF VALOR
978-0-7603-2664-0, 0-7603-2664-9

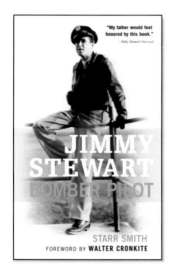

**JIMMY STEWART:
BOMBER PILOT**
978-0-7603-2199-7, 0-7603-2199-X